AF409564

GAME OVER

WHEN THE HEART TRULY AWAKENS

Dr. Michael Stone Ph.d

Dr. Joan Waters Ph.d

ACKNOWLEDGEMENTS

First i acknowledge The Creator and thank The

Creator.

I thank Mother & Father **Mary & Richard P** . memory of
Natashia (Tea) & Phyllis Bradley. Special Thanks to my
Mother who always

To the only Brother i grew up knowing **(Larry Pitts)**
And to his mother **(Amelia Pitts)** who was ALWAYS my
second mother, i thank you and love you both as you've always
loved me unconditionally and never turned your back on me.
LAUREL HATTIX : Thank you for your kindness, guidance &
inspiration during the hardest times of my life.
MRS ANGIE SETZER : Thank you for compassion ,patience,
& devotion during the hardest times of my life. You are the best
lawyer in the world.
Lady Patton : You were a calming force of genuine care &
concern in my life during the hardest times of my life. Thank you.
Mrs Deborah Goodwin : Thank you for your kindness
and genuine understanding during the hardest times a
person has to face.
**Lady Tonya : You were a light & true person during
the hard times. Thank you.**
 To my friend (Ms Adrian) and inspirational light in my life you are
loved and appreciated, you made this possible with your constant
advice and information.,
**Demarcus Shavers (Marquis),Yeah its the Professor back in the
lab ..stay strong and maintain.,**
**My brother - Glenn (ICE)Jackson you are loved brother couldn't
Forget about you Keep that strong mind until the end of time &
we're definitely moving now. Thanks for everything bro., Lil E (**

Robert Earl), Rob Lo(Much love), Psi Dog, Yab, Queen (Quincetta Cargill).

The old PL.25 ((P.Lewis Quarters) Fam. Deborah Goodin, Sophia Wilson, Candice Goodin, Marcus Porter, Donald Dorsey, Victoria Dorsey,

Angela Dorsey, (Polyester) Ester Joe Redman, Kevin Byrd & Jerry Richardson (RIP), Boot (Wherever you are), Cora Mathews, Lady Denise,

Last but not least to the Stealth Ones. The 781ILLUMINATI. The False light of False knowledge is being Faded.

INTRODUCTION

Love is one of the most highly used words in the realm of human interactions but very few actually know what love is and even fewer care to know.

As if it couldn't get any worse there exists the bigger dilemma of there having NEVER been any real or substantial definition given by anyone in modern times.

If one looks, they will discover a vast innumerable amount of books and videos online and in book stores. promoting topics about love and other issues relating to love.

If one looks farther, it will be discovered that Facebook, Instagram, and other social platforms are stuffed with messages and videos from innumerable people supposedly offering relationship and love advice.

Topics ranging from rules of love, building healthy relationships and solving dysfunctions in relationships.

At the end of the day they all have 2 things in common. None of them EVER define what love is in and of itself because the authors don't know, therefore barring them from being able to offer any real solution to problems that exist as result of a lack of love and the second thing they all have in common is quite simple, they all belong in the trash.

There's very little that can be found from the ancient past about love. That's not saying it wasn't given in ancient times but it just wasn't a public teaching given to the average person who lived in those ancient civilizations.

Why? Because it was a particular knowledge and understanding that only a select few were qualified to learn by having been initiated into ancient mystery systems of learning.

Although many have come forth to attempt giving definitions of what love is , all of those expressions in one way or another always defined love by the indirect approach of describing actions and feelings while never giving the actual substance of what love is composed of nor where it originates from within the human being.

When it comes to actions and feelings , no matter how one dresses them up , they are nothing more than the effects of love's function , not a description or definition of its very nature.

This book's purpose is to finally provide that definition as well as help the reader to be able to discover the very heart of all dysfunctions that arise out of not only just a lack of knowledge and understanding about love but a lack of true knowledge and understanding about one's self.

Just think , if the love of self must come first before you can love others , then surely not knowing self poses a greater dysfunction within itself that impedes the facilitation of love.

It is for that very reason that love is accompanied by race & gender identity in these writings so that a greater understanding of love can be realized through a thorough examination of its very nature and how it naturally manifests itself through numerous conduits such as gender and racial identity.

The idea that identity plays a part in anything dealing with love may seem strange and out of place. It may even seem ridiculous and not of major significance.

To surprise you and maybe even shock you, identity is a foundational cornerstone of love from which all other degrees and expressions of love will flow from and through.

The lack of this identity factor is the main cause of things such poor self-esteem, self-hatred, self-destructiveness , self-delusion, and self-devaluation .

All of which impede self-love as a major dysfunction within itself that initiates other dysfunctions.

Since everyone's attention and focus is always on how love applies exclusively to their male/female relationships to the exclusion of everything else, these writings deal exclusively with that particular venue of love first and foremost.

Although that particular venue is dealt with first and foremost , don't underestimate it because it simultaneously reveals some very surprising and unavoidable things about the greater scope of love's power and natural direction that will subtly force you to reexamine all that you thought you knew and understood about yourself and love.

As you continue to read, you find yourself becoming submerged further and further into a whole new world that exists beneath and behind all of the shallow things you may have heard or read about love and yourself.

Like no other before it, this book will be seen by its reader as putting words to things that have been felt or always on the edge of one's conscious mind but never materializing.

The core of the material approaches the subject of love from numerous dimensions in reference to all of the human relations such as friendships, relationships , family , and marriage as it applies to Black People.

What will grab your attention and make it impossible for you to stop reading is the unique grasp and implementation of various previously unknown principles of thought , life , and existence.

The methods employed within these pages not only expose the Black mainstream leadership as a fraud with baseless concepts and theologies that have always falsified an intent to fix the dysfunctional relations amongst Black People.

The methodology will as well expose them as never intending to give Black People the whole truth in the first place.

As psychology is basically nothing more than a field of guess knowledge with no true foundation to ever bring a true model of a Black Nation into reality.

As the field of Psychology currently exists, it is and always will be useless in regards to truly healing and fixing the dysfunctions within the Black family structure and Black race dynamics.

The question that many Blacks have failed to ask themselves is , how could any so-called science from a world that hates them, ever produce something to help them to think right or healthy?

There is presently a continuum of utter failure in regards to anyone resurrecting Black People into an actual collective functioning Nation.

That continuum rests upon an artificially and deceptively manufactured condition of an inner void meant to cause a disconnect from one's true self and any active potential to know , understand and demonstrate love.

That which our complete and universal history of identity was and is meant to show us, has been misdirected and redefined away from us by an elite subterfuge perpetuated by both historical and present day Black thinkers , psychologists , scholars, historians , and religious leaders.

In one way or another this group of people have all sought to indoctrinate us with watered-down theologies of self-knowledge and self-love while none of them have ever come forth to define the exact essence of love and its ultimate nature , function , and significance in the healing of the Black Female/Male relationships, and the Black family structure.

None of these classes of people have ever actually defined The Black race according to its full and complete capacity.

The main method used by so many has always been the vulture approach, to approach the dead carcass of things in the past and seek to define that as the whole of Black People's identity.

Within this book it will be proven with indisputable principles of fact of how that is incorrect and an intentional misrepresentation and dissecting of the complete truth.

The reader will find a wide range of significant topics within these pages and every one of them hits hard and primarily goes to the very heart of what is called The Black Race, the actual dysfunctions within the black family structure, Black relationships, and reveals the never before expressed principles of what a nation (Race) is composed of and the Ultimate reason behind the Europeans destruction of Non-European knowledge bases.

The Ultimate purpose behind these writings is to inspire deeper and more meaningful thought and action in regards to self , one's people and a common enemy that is universal in approach and execution of camouflaged apex tactics from multiple directions.

If nothing else is learned and realized, I hope that two principles are learned, realized, and embedded deep with the mind as a guiding standard of all future endeavors

1.) " **It is a delusional thought of a self- inflicted nature to think, feel, and believe that anything given or taken from an oppressor or conqueror will ever enlighten you or liberate you beyond the boundaries set by them.**"

2.) "**Until a people actually truly understands the greater significance and power of their so-called female within their Nation (Race), the Nation (Race) will continue to be at the mercy of those of another oppressive race who do know and understand it** "

In the course of our living in lands all across the world that are ruled by our conquerors, we have to be careful not to prejudge our histories throughout the earth through the limited, out of context, and naturally biased lenses of the nation and culture in which we live.

Why? because the two substances and the two different natures from which each originate are as diametrically opposed to each other as is oil to water.

Oil and water simply cannot and will not combine unless by an artificial means that by nature is a lie or a distortion of the contexts.

Similarly , in few words, a lion can be displaced out of its natural habitat and environment then be made to exist within the context of a caged environment under a new man-made standard of being right, appropriate, or okay

Why, because it serves the purpose of a trifling intent bent on altering the nature of things from their natural order to satisfy a unnatural mentality.

A mentality originating from the nature of an artificial man who hates all natural things.

Does the indirect creation of salmonella and its growing appearance in everything by tampering with the natures of food sound familiar? How about Chicken flu crossing over into another species (Cows) by the same tampering with the nature of things ? Sound familiar again?

Many believe that finances is the answer to the race problem in America and the world.

That may sound good but the systematic order of Global racism cares nothing about any individual who becomes wealthy, it's what is done with the wealth in regards to a people's total independence and self-preservation within an oppressive nation that will provoke a beast out of its lair to reveal to you the extent of its true nature that a limited knowledge mislead you into thinking, believing, feeling, and foolishly hoping that it possessed only one face, when in fact it was hydra.

These writings are the result of a 20 + year in depth study and research and actually are a part of a much extensive volume of writings called the (Killuminati: The Rise & Demise of The PuppetMasters) which is forthcoming in the near future.

Unlike any other book before its time, the overall material represents principle foundations of existence that none can defy or take an alternative route around.

CHAPTER 1

EMERGENCY ALERT !!!
Change Is Necessary

Difficulties, Problems, & Dissatisfaction In Our Lives is Only A Sign From Life That Changes Are Required

It's easy to declare a desire for change, whether in our personal lives, relationships, or habits.

We often say we want to improve, but our actions can reveal the opposite, suggesting that we're not truly committed to transformation.

This discrepancy between a supposed desire and action exposes a deeper resistance to change, rooted in fear, comfort, or ingrained patterns.

On the surface, wanting change seems simple. We recognize areas that need improvement whether it's health, mental well-being, or the quality of our relationships.

We may feel a strong emotional pull to become better, envisioning the benefits of this transformation.

However, while words express the desire, actions require an actual effort, commitment, consistency, and the ability to break from the comfort of the the norm that one is accustomed to.

This is where resistance shows itself. Humans are creatures of habit and experience, often preferring the familiar over the unknown, even if the familiar is harmful. A person might, for example, express the desire to quit smoking or get healthier. But if they continue to make choices that either encourage or support their old habits like buying cigarettes it suggests that, on a deeper level, they may not truly want the change they claim to seek.

It's easier to stay within the boundaries of what we know than to venture into uncomfortable territory, where the effort and the discomfort of real transformation lie.

Furthermore, the mind often works in subtle ways to sabotage change. We may rationalize our behavior, making excuses for why we haven't acted differently. "I'll start tomorrow" or "It's just one time" are common self-deceptions that keep us locked in old patterns. This inner conflict reveals the power of cognitive incongruity which is tension between what we say we want and what we actually do.

True change requires not just a desire but a willingness to (act) consistently in accordance with that the desire, even when it's difficult. It's a process that involves more than words; it demands self-discipline, sacrifice, and a readiness to confront the underlying fears or attachments that hold us back.

For example, someone may claim they want a healthier relationship, but if they continue engaging in the same toxic dynamics or refusing to work on communication or cultivating positive and nurturing qualities, it becomes clear that the idea of change was more appealing than the reality of doing what it takes to achieve it.

The gap between wanting and doing often reveals that we are not fully committed to the change we claim to desire.

In many cases, we may desire the outcome but are unwilling to endure the process. This unwillingness can be linked to fear of failure, fear of success, or even an identity tied to old habits and ways of being. Thus, while it's easy to say we want change, our actions are a more honest reflection of our readiness to actually pursue it.

Ultimately, real change comes from aligning intention with action. It requires a conscious effort to break free from the habits that keep us stagnant and to continuously move toward growth, even when the path is uncomfortable.

Words can inspire, but only actions lead to true transformation. It's common to express a desire for change, yet many find themselves acting in ways that contradict this. While we might say we want to improve an aspect of our lives whether it's breaking a bad habit, mending a relationship, or pursuing a goal ,our actions often tell a different story.

This contradiction points to a deeper issue: the resistance to the discomfort that real change requires.

One of the main reasons for this resistance is that change disrupts the familiar.

Even when the familiar is negative, such as unhealthy habits or toxic relationships, it feels safer than the uncertainty that comes with change.

For example, someone may say they want to stop procrastinating, but they continue engaging in distractions. This behavior indicates that, despite their words, they are more comfortable with the short-term gratification than the effort and discipline needed for change.

Cognitive dissonance also plays a significant role. We experience a mental conflict when our actions don't align with our intentions, but rather than confronting this, we often rationalize and justify our behavior. Phrases like " It's just for a little while " or " It's just a little bit " help us avoid the discomfort of facing our true resistance to change. These excuses prevent real progress, as we're stuck in a loop of wanting change but doing the opposite.

True transformation requires not only the desire for change but also the willingness to face discomfort and break free from ingrained patterns. It's easy to say we want something, but unless our actions support that desire consistently, we're not fully committed. Real change happens when we align our intentions with consistent effort, no matter how uncomfortable or challenging the process may be.

Many of us claim to desire change, yet resist the actual process because it demands a shift in mindset. Real change isn't just about altering behaviors; it requires confronting long-held beliefs, fears, ideas and habits that exist as the source of the actions that keep us comfortable in the familiar.

This mental resistance often sabotages our intentions, as we fear the discomfort and uncertainty that come with transformation.

We might say we want to change, but deep down, we cling to the mindset that keeps us stuck, avoiding the hard work of mental reprogramming necessary for true, lasting change.

Sometimes, we don't achieve the change we desire because we are not fully prepared to embrace the deep, internal shifts that change demands.

While we might think we want something—whether it's a healthier lifestyle, better relationships, or personal growth—our actions often reveal hesitation or even resistance.

This contradiction stems from a deeper issue: achieving real change requires more than simply wanting it; it requires altering our mindset and our relationship with discomfort.

One key reason we fail to achieve change is our attachment to comfort and familiarity. Change disrupts routines and challenges long-held beliefs or habits, and even when these habits are unproductive or harmful, they provide a sense of security.

For instance, a person may express a desire to break free from a toxic relationship, but if they continue making the same counter-productive choices or returning to the same dynamics, it's a sign they're clinging to what's familiar.

The fear of stepping into the unknown, where new habits and perspectives must be built, must at some point be overcome and repositioned to outweigh the perceived discomfort of that which is new and the continuance in an undesirable situation.

Our minds are also powerful in maintaining the norms that rest as the source of our dissatisfactions.

When we face the challenge of change, cognitive dissonance—the tension between what we want and what we actually do—can cause us to rationalize inaction. We might tell ourselves, "I'll change this or that tomorrow," or "I can handle this one time," effectively delaying the change we claim to desire.

This mental self-sabotage keeps us stuck, as we avoid the difficult work of truly transforming our thoughts and behaviors. Moreover, real change requires a mindset shift, which is one of the hardest parts of the process. It's not enough to change on the surface; we must challenge the beliefs and thought patterns that got us stuck in the first place.

For example, someone may want to become more confident, but unless they confront and shift the limiting thoughts, ideas, and beliefs that have kept them insecure, they won't experience lasting change to any significant degree.

Ultimately, the gap between wanting change and achieving it often lies in our unwillingness to leave behind the mental and emotional comfort of old patterns. True transformation comes when we not only desire change but are also willing to embrace the discomfort and uncertainty of growth. Without this commitment to altering our mindset, we remain in the same place, no matter how much we say we want things to be different.

Many people fail to realize that true change requires embracing something different—whether it's new information, different perspectives, or new actions.

This is often why we remain stuck in the same loops and cycles of thought and behavior. It's tempting to believe that just wanting change or thinking about it is enough.

However, if we continue to approach our challenges with the same mindset and actions that created them, we inevitably stay within the same patterns.

Real change comes from exposing ourselves to something outside of our usual myopic standards ,perceptions ,routines and habits.

For example, we may want to improve our relationships, but if we keep responding to conflict in the same ways, we're unlikely to scc improvement or if we continue to base our conclusions and decisions upon superficial external attractions, we're highly unlikely to ever find a true relation or experience that is founded upon the true inner elements of mind and heart (where love exists).

To break these cycles, we need to approach situations with a different mindset or learn new ways of communicating and responding. This requires us to engage with unfamiliar or uncomfortable practices that challenge our current knowledge, understanding , and behavior.

Similarly, change often requires the intake of new, informative material. When we receive fresh knowledge or insights—

whether through books, therapy, or conversations—it opens up new pathways in our minds.

This knowledge can help us see the flaws in our previous thinking or behaviors and present us with actionable steps toward growth.

Without exposing ourselves to different information, we often reinforce the same beliefs that have kept us stuck.

Beyond just thinking differently, real change demands new actions that only a new knowledge, new understanding,and a new thought process can create.

Many people fall into the trap of believing that understanding the need for change is the same as taking the steps to achieve it. The reality is that even with the right information, if our actions don't change, neither will our outcomes.

It's not enough to stay within the comfort zone of familiar behaviors; true transformation happens when we make different, often uncomfortable choices that break old patterns.

For instance, if someone wants to become more disciplined, they might need to change their daily routine in a way that pushes them out of their habitual comfort, like waking up earlier or adopting a new practice.

In essence, change requires us to break out of our established cycles—both mentally and behaviorally. It's in the shift from familiar thinking and actions to something new and unfamiliar that real growth takes place. Staying in the same loop, repeating the same behaviors, and feeding the same thought patterns will only lead to the same results.

True change involves stepping outside of what we know, embracing new ideas, and taking actions that push us into new territory. Without this shift, we simply remain in a cycle of wanting change but never achieving it.

When it comes to change there is one important factor that must be realized, nothing is created perfect from the beginning or perfected from the beginning, there are always stages of development involved that require us to take one step at a time and this necessitates patience and focused effort with the small things that eventually accumulate together into something big and significant being accomplished.

There will always be something that needs immediate change depending upon the degree of discomfort, danger, or dissatisfaction

Involved. This kind of change requires some form of planning beforehand so that the immediate results from the immediate action will give us some kind of mental and emotional room of peace and stability to further think in an unobstructed beginning of a new mindstate and environment.

The most important factor to keep in mind is that the degree of change will always be determined by the degree of thought, planning, will power ,confidence, and effort that we invest into our desired changes.

Chapter 2

Change Part 2 : Blaming Others For What We Allowed Or Encouraged Them To Do

Personal transformation is the key to resolving the recurring issues we face in our connections with others.

Blaming external factors or other people often shifts focus from the real work…changing ourselves.

At the heart of every relationship is our ability to make choices: how we choose to allow others to approach us , how we approach others, and what we seek in them and why.

Too often, our dissatisfaction stems from chasing external or superficial qualities such as looks and material things, neglecting the importance of inner values and deeper compatibility.

By shifting our focus inward, we gain the clarity to make decisions based on genuine alignment rather than fleeting attraction or societal expectations. This process requires self-awareness and accountability; it's about acknowledging that we cannot control others, but we can always control ourselves, choose how we respond, engage, and grow within our relationships.

If we cultivate this inner change….working on our emotional intelligence, personal values, and understanding of what truly matters, we are better equipped to enter relationships from a place of strength ,clarity and true inner definition.

Instead of perpetuating cycles of dysfunction by repeating the same patterns of behavior or attaching to the wrong people, we can either choose wisely or recognize when to walk away from a relationship that isn't serving our true self.

Ultimately, the power lies within us to create healthier dynamics by shifting our focus from blaming others to nurturing our own growth and understanding.

This inward transformation allows us to discern between relationships that nourish our growth and those that detract from it, empowering us to make the right choices with confidence and precision.

To effectively discern the potential for growth and nurturing within a person before initiating a relationship, it is crucial to transform our thinking and analytical processes.

This change involves adopting a more reflective and discerning approach to evaluating individuals.

Instead of reacting to initial impressions or superficial traits, we should cultivate a deeper understanding of our values and goals, applying this insight to assess compatibility with potential partners.

By refining our analytical framework, we move beyond surface-level attractions or societal expectations and focus on whether a person aligns with our core values ,aims, purposes and aspirations.

This involves questioning how well they support our personal growth, share similar goals, and contribute to our well-being. Such an approach requires a shift from impulsive judgments to a more defined and deliberate, values-driven evaluation. Embracing this thoughtful analysis empowers us to make informed decisions from the outset, positioning us to enter relationships that offer mutual support and growth.

By prioritizing self-awareness and intentional evaluation, we can better identify individuals who contribute positively to our lives, ultimately fostering healthier and more fulfilling connections. This proactive stance not only enhances our chances of finding nurturing relationships but also saves us from potential dissatisfaction , hurt, and misalignment.

Unrealistic Expectations

Expanding further regarding self-delusional and unrealistic expectations, it's important to address how our tendency to blame others for our disappointments often stems from a lack of self-awareness and an insufficient analysis of the nature and inequalities within a person's mind and heart. This self-delusion arises when we project our own unmet needs and desires onto others, expecting them to fulfill roles or meet standards that may not be realistic or fair.

When we blame others for our dissatisfaction, we are often masking our own shortcomings in understanding or evaluating relationships. This failure to deeply analyze a person's compatibility with our values and emotional needs leads us to form unrealistic expectations. For instance, we might expect a partner to be consistently supportive or emotionally available without considering whether their true nature aligns with our expectations.

The crux of this issue lies in our tendency to focus on surface-level traits or initial attractions rather than engaging in a thorough assessment of how well a person's values, emotional capacity, and life goals align with our own.

This oversight results in unrealistic expectations, where we hope someone will change or adapt to fit an idealized version of what we want them to be.

Such self-delusion perpetuates a cycle of disappointment and blame, as we fail to recognize that our dissatisfaction often stems from our own unrealistic projections rather than the other person's inherent flaws. By not taking the time to understand the deeper aspects of a person's mind and heart, we set ourselves up for failure in relationships.

We are essentially seeking to fulfill our emotional needs through others without ensuring they are genuinely capable of meeting those needs.

To break this cycle, we must cultivate a habit of honest self-reflection and realistic expectation-setting. This involves examining our own values, needs, and goals and then assessing potential partners against these criteria. We should focus on whether a person's attributes and behaviors genuinely support and enhance our growth, rather than idealizing them based on superficial or temporary qualities.

This approach requires a commitment to understanding both ourselves and others more deeply.

By confronting and addressing our self-delusional thoughts and expectations, we position ourselves to make more informed and realistic decisions about who to pursue in relationships.

Ultimately, this self-awareness and rigorous analysis allow us to form connections that are more aligned with our true needs and desires, leading to more fulfilling and equitable relationships.

The Lack Of The Ability Or Willingness To Question Others

When it comes to broken relationships, marriages, friendships, and family relations where we believe that others have tricked us, hurt us, used us, or disrespected our trust and loyalty, most times we completely blame the others while scapegoating our own part in it that gave others the power and opportunity to do what they did to us.

Our inability and lack of willpower to question others' motives and definitions about the most significant aspects of life leaves us vulnerable to deception, shaping our perceptions and actions in ways we might not realize.

This phenomenon operates at a personal, social, and even cultural level, subtly altering our decisions, beliefs, and relationships.

At its core, this vulnerability stems from two intertwined human tendencies: the desire for comfort and the fear of confrontation.

We often avoid questioning others about their true understanding of things, intentions or the meaning behind their words, particularly when it comes to matters that hold deep significance—such as love, trust, and personal success.

By taking others' statements at face value, we are lulled into a sense of security.

For instance, when a person professes affection or loyalty without us ever probing deeper into their understanding of those terms, we may assume they align with our own desires, wants , or needs.

In reality, however, these expressions and their true intent often differ widely from one's own, leading to misunderstandings, broken relationships, or feelings of betrayal.

The deception arises not just from the other person's motives but from our failure to challenge or investigate their definitions and be patient enough to observe the consistency or inconsistency of their actions over an extended period of time.

Furthermore, the fear of damaging relationships often prevents us from pushing harder for clarity. Confronting or questioning someone about their understanding, motives or definitions about things can feel uncomfortable or even confrontational, especially when we are attracted to the person or hold a deep emotional connection with that person.

This reluctance creates a fertile environment for manipulation, where ambiguity in intentions, a lack of definition or vague definitions become tools for deceit. For instance, someone might take advantage of our trust by operating within this ambiguity, acting in ways that benefit them while we remain unaware of their true intentions.

Another contributing factor is the social pressure to conform. Society often encourages us to avoid confrontation and accept others' statements without question to maintain harmony.

This norm is particularly pervasive in close-knit relationships, where challenging or questioning someone's definitions or motives may be viewed as a sign of mistrust or disrespect. In such situations, we choose not to ask difficult questions to avoid discomfort, but this choice paves the way for deception.

For example, in friendships or partnerships, one party might exploit the other's unwillingness to question their behaviors, allowing selfish motives to go unchecked.

Further more, a lack of introspection often accompanies this inability to question.

We may not take the time to reflect on our own values, beliefs, and definitions, much less challenge or require others to do the same. Without a strong foundation in our own understanding, it becomes even easier to adopt the perspectives or interpretations of others without questioning them.

This passive acceptance of others' views opens us up to being deceived about what truly matters.

In conclusion, our reluctance to question others' motives and definitions—whether due to discomfort, fear of confrontation, or societal pressures—sets the stage for deception.

By failing to probe deeper, we allow others' intentions and definitions to shape our lives in ways that may not serve us, leaving us vulnerable to manipulation.

To guard against this, it is essential to develop the courage and willpower to ask the difficult questions that reveal the truth behind others' words and actions.

The inability and lack of willpower to question others often stem from a deep-rooted fear of being confronted with our own limitations about that which we may choose to present questions about.

The one main unrevealed vulnerability that most people guard about themselves when it comes to life's most important and significant things such as love is that very little or nothing is known or understood by us about love but we project a highly sophisticated illusion to others as if we do and fear the moment of being questioned so the resulting course of action is to never present questions about love to others out of the fear of being questioned in return by the questioned ones.

When we shy away from asking difficult questions, it isn't just a reflection of a reluctance to challenge or question the external expressions of others, but also an avoidance of facing our own ignorance.

The fear of not knowing the answers creates an internal conflict where we prioritize comfort over truth. This hesitancy fuels dysfunction in our decision-making and our perception of reality, as we allow deceptive narratives to go unquestioned, and unchallenged.

By avoiding difficult questions, we maintain the illusion of stability, but this very avoidance opens the door for further manipulation and deception.

Deceptive thinking and scheming individuals exploit this vulnerability by feeding us answers and things they think or know we want to hear that go unquestioned, reinforcing the cycle of deception.

Furthermore, when we choose not to question others, we also deny ourselves the opportunity for growth.

The act of questioning not only challenges external knowledge but forces us to reckon with our own gaps in understanding. It is this confrontation with our own uncertainty that many find extremely uncomfortable. Yet, the discomfort of not knowing is the very fuel for emotional ,intellectual and spiritual progress. By not engaging in this process, we remain passive participants in our own deception, facilitating the influence and control others exert over us.

In short, our inability to question stems from an unwillingness to admit our ignorance, and this reluctance perpetuates dysfunction and deception in all spheres of life.

True liberation lies in embracing the difficult process of inquiry, even when it reveals our own limitations.

The ultimate reality that can have no valid argument against it is that if someone is truly genuine, sincere , and possessing positive and rightful intentions, they should have no problem with being questioned or analyzed.

The genuine, sincere, and honest at heart actually view the act of being questioned or analyzed as nothing more than an welcomed opportunity to prove themselves as being exactly what and who they've presented and represented themselves as being.

Those hard hitting questions that should be asked are coming later.

Chapter 3

Emotional Insanity: Looking For Something While Not Knowing What You're Looking For

Many individuals tend to idolize specific life situations or aspirations without a comprehensive understanding of what those goals truly entail or what process was involved to produce those things.

This norm can be attributed to several psychological and social factors, including the allure of superficial aspects and the influence of societal and peer ideals.

People often envision success or happiness in relationships or finances based on idealized images presented by media, cultural narratives, or even peer experiences, without delving into the complexities and challenges involved.

Firstly, the media plays a significant role in shaping and distorting perceptions of success. Television shows, movies, and social media platforms frequently portray glamorous lifestyles or extraordinary achievements in a simplified and idealized manner. These portrayals can lead individuals to form unrealistic expectations and aspirations without considering the real-life struggles and sacrifices required to attain them. The disconnect between the idealized image and actual experience can result in disillusionment and frustration when reality does not meet these expectations.

Secondly, cultural and societal pressures often contribute to the idealization of certain life situations. Societal standards and norms can create a narrow definition of success or happiness, leading people to chase after these ideals without understanding their true implications.

For instance, the pursuit of wealth, fame, or status is often depicted as the ultimate goal, yet achieving these objectives may not necessarily lead to fulfilment or contentment.

The focus on superficial markers of success can overshadow the importance of personal values and individual needs.

Furthermore, the lack of in-depth knowledge about the realities of these idealized goals can result in a superficial understanding of the challenges involved. Individuals may be drawn to the end result without considering the underlying effort, mistakes, commitment, and potential drawbacks that were involved in the middle of the process before the results were produced.

For example, aspiring to be a successful entrepreneur might overlook the significant risks, financial uncertainties, and personal sacrifices associated with starting and running a business. The romanticized vision of entrepreneurship can mask the harsh and sometimes frustrating realities of the entrepreneurial journey.

To mitigate this phenomenon, it is essential for individuals to engage in thorough research and self-reflection before pursuing idealized aspirations.

By seeking a realistic understanding of the demands and consequences associated with their goals, individuals can make more informed decisions and set achievable expectations.

Additionally, fostering a mindset that values personal growth and intrinsic satisfaction over societal and other external validations can help individuals align their aspirations with their true values and needs.

In conclusion, the idealization of certain life situations or aspirations without a comprehensive understanding of their realities is a common phenomenon driven by media influence, societal pressures, peer influences, and superficial perceptions.

Addressing this issue requires a more realistic approach to goal-setting, one that emphasizes realistic expectations and personal alignment with genuine values. By doing so, individuals can better navigate their intentions, desires, and goals and find more meaningful and fulfilling paths in life.

Wanting or Desiring Something Without Considering or Knowing The Total Extent Of What It Consists Of & Requires

The lack of in-depth knowledge and understanding about the things we claim to want often results in a pattern of indecision and frequent shifts in our life choices.

When individuals are drawn to idealized goals or aspirations without grasping their true nature, they may find themselves making numerous, often conflicting decisions.

This indecisiveness stems from a superficial comprehension of what these goals entail, leading to a continual re-evaluation and alteration of one's path.

For instance, someone who idolizes the idea of a high-powered career may initially pursue it with enthusiasm. However, without understanding the full scope of the job's demands, such as long hours and high stress, they might later feel overwhelmed and dissatisfied.

This lack of foresight can prompt them to pivot towards different career options in search of something that better aligns with their expectations, only to encounter similar issues. This cycle of chasing and shifting reflects a deeper issue: the failure to fully comprehend the realities behind the aspirations.

This phenomenon is often fueled by an incomplete or idealized understanding of what one desires.

Movie, television and media portrayals also societal narratives provide simplified or distorted images of success and fulfillment, leading individuals to chase after these illusions.

When reality does not match these idealized expectations, the resulting frustration and confusion can drive a person to continuously alter their goals and decisions.

Moreover, the constant shifting of choices can prevent individuals from making substantial progress in any one area. Without a solid foundation of knowledge and understanding, it becomes challenging to commit to a single path, leading to a fragmented and unfulfilled journey through life.

Addressing this issue requires a deeper introspection and a realistic assessment of one's true desires and the demands or requirements they consist of.

Only by developing a thorough understanding of what we truly want can we make more decisive and consistent choices, leading to a more coherent and satisfying path in life.

CHAPTER 4

Game Over : Undeceiving The Deceived & Unloved

In the world, individuals often find themselves caught up or trapped in a complex web of emotional turmoil and dissatisfaction.

This phenomenon is particularly pronounced in those who lack a clear definition and understanding about the objects of their desires, instead articulating superficial aspects of their wants without any true or significant definition of things that in reality mask deeper insecurities and confusion.

The inability to accurately define the object of one's desires such as love creates a fertile ground for deception, as individuals become vulnerable to misleading images and words presented by others, ultimately perpetuating their emotional disarray.

At the core of this issue lies a fundamental disconnect between what individuals believe they want and their actual position of not knowing or understanding the very dynamic, nature, and process of that which they say or believe they want.

Many people navigate life under the guise of pursuing goals and ambitions that seem appealing on the surface—be it career success, romantic relationships, or social recognition—without the ability or willingness to ever critically analyze and discover the exact nature and elemental properties of that which they've been influenced to think and believe they want.

This disconnection fosters a form of emotional insanity, where individuals become trapped in a cycle of longing for outcomes that ultimately aren't within their ability to find and experience simply because they have no true idea of what it truly is.

This is a playground ruled by deceivers and game players of the heart who are always unquestionably given admittance to the door of sincere but ignorant hearts with just the simple superficial qualification of possessing some superficial as aspect of such as looks or humor that most people find overwhelmingly attractive and just the mention of the mere words of "love" ,"soulmate", or "romantic at heart" that the emotional prey has no ability to analyze or question to determine the validity of due to a lack of not truly knowing or understanding what love truly is.

A lack of introspection leads to a fragmented sense of self, wherein the pursuit of external validation becomes a substitute for internal fulfillment.

The implications of this disconnect are profound. When individuals assert desires that lack true definition, they open themselves to external influences. They become susceptible to persuasive figures—be it marketers, influencers ,charismatic leaders , or players of the heart who exploit this ambiguity for their gain.

These individuals, often skilled in the art of manipulation, present enticing images and narratives that resonate with the superficial wants of those searching for some personal self meaning and direction within life and love.

The emotional landscape of these individuals becomes cluttered with illusions, as they chase after promises that ultimately lead to disillusionment , frustration, disappointment and emotional distress.

Moreover, the inability to question the validity of these external messages and projections heightens the vulnerability and disadvantages of the situation.

Many individuals, lacking a robust framework for discerning truth from deception, are never able to challenge the claims made by those who present themselves as being what another wants and needs.

This creates a perpetual cycle: the more they accept and cling to these deceptive words and projections, the more entrenched they become in their emotional insanity.

Their journey becomes one of chasing shadows, constantly seeking fulfillment in places where it cannot be found, thus perpetuating a cycle of dissatisfaction.

The intersection of emotional insanity and the inability to define the object of one's wants , needs, and pursuits creates a precarious situation for many individuals.

The quest for validation through superficial ideas, perceptions , and wants obscures the path to genuine fulfillment, allowing deceptive narratives to thrive.

To break free from this cycle, individuals must engage in deeper self-reflection, cultivate self-awareness, and challenge the superficial and substanceless societal norms such as movies, television, and peer influences that shaped one's wants and pursuits of the heart according to superficial and illusionary standards and ideas.

By doing so, one can begin to reclaim their emotional well-being and move toward a more genuine and real existence, grounded in a true definitional understanding of the objects of their wants, needs and aspirations. Only through this process can they hope to dispel the illusions that have clouded their vision and find a path toward genuine fulfillment.

The underlying principles of life and reality expresses and demonstrates the simple formula of **symbols and substance** which dictates that in order for a symbol to represent reality, the truth, or that which is right, then the symbol must possess an actual real substance behind it that is congruent with what the symbol represents and proves the symbol as a correct representation of that which is real , true, and able to be experienced as represented.

For example, words are written and sounded symbols that are meant to represent the existence of physical substances like "sand" which represents the existence of a material substance that we know to be on the ground.

Ok what if the word "sand" became altered and was made to represent the substance that we know as "clouds in the sky" ?, then that symbol "sand" would cease to be backed by its correct substance and would become a false representation.

Another example is a concept such as a stop sign.

The Stop sign is a physical representation of a rule or law that means to cease motion in a vehicle but what if someone said that the stop sign personally meant for them to speed up? Would that not be a misinterpretation and misrepresentation of the substance behind the stop sign which is the rule of the road or driving?

What would be the effect of it , would there not be increased crashes if the misrepresentation was followed by everyone?

Would that not be a factual incongruent state between the stop sign and the substance that the person replaced the original rule with? "Stop sign means to speed up"

Those examples relate to the voids we create in reference to love and many of life's other most important things by the uninformed thoughts and perceptions we formulate and the uninformed decisions and actions we make that seek to redefine the natural order and function of things according to uninformed and incorrect personal assumptions which create the heart of all dysfunctions in our lives.

The representation of something without its correct inner substance Is a clear and direct parallel to the reality of love in the lives of people of the world, the word (love) is there but the true substance and meaning of love is not.

How so? Simply by people using the word love and putting whatever they choose behind the word as if it is a true representation of love.

We as people will only grow into a better knowledge and understanding of love only after we learn one of the most hardest lessons in life, anything we as individuals didn't create such as love , can never be just exclusively defined and confined for own personal individual wants or desires.

That is so because love by its very nature doesn't and won't conform to any one's desires , it influences conformity to it so that many can be connected in a state or condition of one accordance that it alone produces and defines.

Love's ultimate purpose is bigger than any one person's desires , thoughts, and expectations, so much so until it produces , incorporates , and influences the existence of stages in how it must be facilitated in order to reach its highest manifestations.

The number one example is where the right Male/Female relationships naturally produce the right family structure and the right family structure produces the right unification and direction of a race (Nation) within love's highest manifestation, a race's (Nation's) collective consciousness.

What the complexities of relationships often reveal are dysfunctional qualities that can challenge even the strongest of bonds.

These issues ranging from breakdowns in communication to unresolved conflicts can hinder the growth and health of all human relations.

All of the negative cycles have occurred for one central reason. **This world has not truly known or understood love.**

These writings emerge to provide hope and new innovative practical solutions for modern relations like friendships , relationships , family , and marriages in a unique way and method that emphasizes the importance of going beyond the ineffective assumptions and theories of the past.

Theories that didn't provide an actual knowledge and understanding of love but rather added to the problems with artificial ideas and academic theories that still remain comparable to this scenario:

"A dog trying to provide a tree with emotional intelligence , empathy, and active listening skills as foundational tools to help the tree help humans to overcome the dysfunction factor in human relations."

The first chapter not only sets the foundation for us to understand the nature of the complexities involving the dysfunctions of human relations in the world but will as well help us to begin to know and understand some very significant things about one's self and what we thought we knew and understood about love.

Ultimately, gaining a deeper understanding of love itself is crucial.

Love is not a feeling or an emotion but actually exists as something much more profound and consequential not only to ourselves but in the way we connect with others.

There are many impediments that either prevent us from receiving love or prevent us from being able to facilitate love in its TRUEST expressions with a solid base of consistency.

In-depth knowledge of love also involves acknowledging and respecting the boundaries that love naturally produces to prevent the occurrence of negative, hurtful , and destructive things from happening.

One of the main questions that these writings answer is a fundamental question that many of us have never been able to answer ourselves ,whether we're willing to admit it or not. "Do you know what love actually is?" Not what it does or how it performs like caring , kind , and etc.

CHAPTER 5

Can Not Exist Within A Void

There is a foolish belief amongst the majority of the world's people that when it comes to our lives, we can just simply approach the foundations of life from any perspective that we choose and the outcome will be the right results.

That same premise also assumes that when it comes to love, we can simply disregard anything that we don't consider relevant to what we're doing or trying to accomplish.

It is by this very approach that we disqualify ourselves from even knowing and understanding love.

One might wonder, how is that possible? Its more than possible because :

1.)   We don't and can't control love.

2.)   Love brings its own definition, method, and function of how to do things

3.)   Love is formatted so that it has to begin with and within an individual first which means that you have to learn to love self (entirely).

The thought, feeling, and actions of loving yourself for who you are isn't easy or as simple as just doing it, to be able to love yourself adds some prerequisites to the whole ordeal where you first have to know who you are as your gender and your race and how that defines you in your individuality.

In most of our minds

, the only thing that matters is the opposite sex that we're chasing or interested in. To most of us that's the only love that we care about and the only one we're truly interested in.

This is the most dominant thought, feeling, and perception of Black people with a few exceptions.

Within this thinking is the underlying idea and assumption that this is where love truly begins.

Its like out of nowhere with no clear justification, we just simply believe we can just simply approach that identity and the production of love from any direction that we choose without there being any requirements of truth as a guide.

In order to give you a simplified analogy of what is being expressed, consider the fact of a seed ,the seed needs things beyond itself in order to grow and until these things like the appropriate environment (dirt or soil) is added , the seed in and of itself cannot and will not grow.

Why? because there are other prerequisites that must be present before the seed can even begin its process of growth and development like water after it has been placed into the dirt.

The lack of water or soil in either case is a void. Unknowingly to most people, love works along similar principles where certain things must be present before it can become awakened.

Then at another stage in its growth as a sprouting seed that has pushed upward above ground, it still needs the soil and water but at this next stage it must have sunlight or it will begin to wither away.

Even in this analogy, according to the knowledge that the average person has about the dirt or soil in the growth process of a seed, it is a highly unknown fact that the soil itself contains certain minerals and elements that must be present within the soil in order for it to even help grow a seed. It is the same with love.

This is seen in certain situations where certain seeds are placed in a soil that has a certain pale color to it with nothing growing from it and the seed is placed in this particular soil and it doesn't even grow at all.

Another analogy is one dealing with a particular building with an advertisement sign over the front of the building that says it's a clothing store and then there is another smaller sign posted on the entrance door that says "Now open for business " but there isn't one single clothing, shoe, or any other retail item inside of the building.

The point is that the building is not an actual clothing store yet and will not truly be open for business or become what it is meant to be until the actual clothing items are placed in the building.

Both of these analogies apply to an identity and love in ways that most people have not even considered.

People can think what they want to think about a racial identity and love all day and continue to only experience the failure of what they assumed was love.

As direct result, the fact shall remain that there will always seem to be something that is missing from those assumed love experiences because there actually is and those things are the contexts through which love must be facilitated in order for it to actually become a true reality in the mind, heart and life of anyone.

The actual foundation of any identity theology must be facilitated through a true and complete perception of Black people that are to be defined according to a certain identity frame.

That identity frame's foundation in no shape, form, or fashion can be given through the context of foreign influences, through the context of a partial knowledge and understanding that seeks to confine the identity to a select few geographical locations when the history of Black People has always existed beyond what Caucasians named Africa.

That identity can not be forced through the reoccuring ignorant context of a blatant disregard for the actual fact that not all Black People have wooly hair and that Black people of Africa are just one branch of the Black Nation tree.

Why and how is that a fact? Because when you take something that is incomplete and try to complete someone with it, what you end up producing is a void or vacuum that holds no true substance by which that person can become the totality of that which they are meant to be.

In other words you only produce and foster a partial identity platform with no means to actuate and activate the fullest potential and capability that a complete identity naturally empowers one with.

On the other hand, if what you attempt to define a people's identity by, is false and unreal, then all you'll be doing in the end is once again producing a void or vacuum but from this false platform, the void or vacuum will handicap people from being able to correctly perceive themselves , function, and react within the fabric and context of reality and truth.

There is one main context that remains either intentionally ignored or unrealized which presents astronomical consequences that hinder and prevent the existence of Black Unity and love from occurring in a more complete and more fulfilling form on a universal scale throughout the world.

That context is the state and condition of the very nature of the society , countries, and world that we live in.

The present order of the world along with all of its faculties of learning and the systems that derived from it is the result of conquerors and all conquerors had one main thing in common, to either destroy, hide or distort anything with a unifying nature to it because all conquerors came to divide people and the most effective method was eliminating or distorting the knowledge of who those people were so that they could be maintained in a fractualized existence by the only unified force, that of the conqueror.

Identity was the first casualty of war ,then came LOVE ,thus the elimination of a context through which love naturally manifests itself like the true identity and power of who so-called females actually are.

The knowledge of the people's identity, nature and power of the Nation or race had to destroyed or hidden because that knowledge and understanding produced love in its largest and most powerful manifestation, the family unit (the result of proper female/ male relationships).

Without such, a void exists that rests as the origins of racism's power to effect and control the targeted groups of racism and rests as the origins of sexism's power to define and confine a certain class of gender to an overall position of inferiority which happens to originate from the same source.

The true nature of both racism and sexism are division tools that prevents love from being active in all avenues of human existence with a universal love effect.

In the world of psychology, academic theories , and religion people are prone to think , believe , and express the idea that something is wrong with the way in which people either think and act or don't think and act.

This is always said as though that is getting at the very heart of the dysfunctions in human relations or as if that is telling the whole truth about the way people think and how they came to think a certain way.

In fact it is something totally different, much deeper, and more crucial to the facilitating of Love by humans than anything else and that particular thing is the state, quality, and condition of the actual human beings mindstate and the uninformed norms that has influenced it to be that way.

The world of psychology , Academic Theory , and religion proposes to fix everything dealing with humans while in and of themselves not possessing an actual knowledge and understanding of the human being itself , thereby making it impossible for the world of psychology ,Academic Theory ,and religion to fix something that they do not have an actual and factual knowledge and understanding about.

What does that actually mean?

It means that in accordance with facts, an individual in and of themselves aren't the essential representation of themselves, an individual is the prime result of a process that defines him or her.

That particular process is best termed as a context in which a particular thing is defined by nature and a particular context in which a particular thing behaves according to that nature.

Principles of truth and right are foundational contexts through which love manifests and expresses itself. This is something that may make some people feel uncomfortable or angry because it's a norm for many to think and feel they can lie and deceive and yet remain a perfect facilitator of love.

In the world of reality, there's no such thing as a little white lie or a partial liar and deceiver.

If you aren't disciplined enough to not lie and tell even an occasional lie, you're a liar. There's no in-between line that allows you to be both at the same time. "An honest person" is a definite and conclusive title that signifies the nonexistence of a lie or deceit. The moment the words or act of deception happens, the person is no longer "an honest person." Contrary to what most people think and believe, there's no such thing as an honest person being honest in one area but not others.

That person is only one capable of truth while possessing an inclination to lie. Thus a liar and not totally honest.

Why? Because of one main principle:

The Principle of position and occupying space :

"No two objects can occupy the same space at one time. Likewise a lie and truth can not co-exist together. They are two opposing natures that can't occupy the same place at the same time. "

Love can't and won't exist within a lie.

The inclination to lie doesn't and won't just effect certain areas, its nature causes a fluctuation or void in one's ability to facilitate love because love by its very nature influences and solidifies consistency.

If you have a world that has been built upon the distortion of truth , the hiding of truth and deception about truth, why wouldn't the same world seek to distort the truth, hide the truth , and be deceptive about the one principal foundational element that exclusively defines, produces, and directs the course of human nature and human potential? The so-called female?

Through such deception, there's no way that any female would have knowledge of who she actually is and what that actually entails as far as the nature of a female and the unequaled natural power, abilities and purposes that go with it.

Being female is a context through which love manifests and expresses itself and so is male and Race a context through which love manifests and expresses itself.

The lack of knowledge and understanding of these contexts and numerous others are prerequisite conditions that have made love impossible on any significant large scale throughout the world.

This is one of the major misunderstandings about love.

In a unnatural world, people naturally have the unnatural notion that love only applies to that which immediately affects them or immediately serves
their particular individual self-interests.

This is a predominant misperception that most people have as though individuals have the unquestionable right and power to define and confine love within the set perimeter of who they are and what they want, to the exclusion of others that are not immediately connected to them.

Contrary to popular thought or feeling, love never confines itself to any particular limitations or specific areas.

Love in all of its magnificent and indomitable power by nature seeks to encompass each and every avenue of human thought and behavior, nature around us, and the universe as the exclusive means by which it as the ultimate definer and director of all, assigns degrees of positive and powerful results to all things according to how much a thing is in accordance with the nature in which it was created.

Simply meaning, the degree to which a thing is in accordance or direct alignment with its nature determines a thing's degree of access to its natural abilities and a prescribed degree of power with a natural balance that gives a high degree of efficiency and sufficiency in all that it conceives, intends, and performs.

Why? How? Because that is the apex definition that determines whether a thing is right or wrong.

According to that same principle of nature, the degree to which a thing is out of accordance or alignment with its nature determines the degree to which it lacks access to its natural abilities and produces an imbalance (dysfunction) that prescribes either a low or non-existent efficient and proficiency level within all that it conceives, intends, or performs towards positivity.

Most people who are out of alignment with their nature have a high tendency towards producing negative thoughts and situations that effect others in a counterproductive way although the thoughts and situations may serve their own interests quite well but only at the cost of disregarding the needs and feelings of others.

Why? or How? Because that is the apex of being wrong.

Thus is explained the principle essence of the world's dysfunctional human relations. Namely sexism and racism where people want to define the nature and function of other beings according to their will and standards.

Like the Male redefining the so-called female's position, role, and power according to an unnatural egotistical masculine desire to be superior and to deny the so-called female her equality and superiority in areas that her nature was specifically designed for.

Areas that aren't about physical strength but rests as the very essence of man's physical strength.

Do you men know what the nature and power of a so-called female's nature is? Do you so-called females even know or understand it?

Yeah, it's been said until it's worn out that her nature is to comfort but that's on the extreme outer edges of it.

If one as a so-called female doesn't know or understand what it is, then how can she ever fulfill her natural position or destinies? How can anyone truly understand why there's an imbalance in the family structure and the entire social construct ? And how can one even claim to be able to fix these dysfunctions without having a sufficient knowledge and understanding of the natures of the individuals involved?

The answers are readily observed in the effects of the so-called psychological and religious remedies that all have the imbalanced masculine ego as its origin and have only pacified and enlarged the negative effects of the dysfunctions.

How so? the divorce rates continue to climb even while setting new records in the divorce rate, violence and kidnappings against the so-called females continue to rise at record numbers, child abuse and child neglect continues to rise, the masculine based culture of so-called female disrespect (Hoes, Bixxhes, etc.) continues, abortions continue to rise (The #1 killer of all people of color),Black relationship spans continue to shorten.

That is quite a list of things but not even the tip of the iceberg as the saying goes.

Chapter 6

Reclaiming Yourself For Reconstruction

In today's fast-paced and highly deceptive world, many individuals find themselves being influenced quickly by external pressures that dictate their thoughts, emotions, and spiritual beliefs.

These influences can stem from societal expectations, cultural norms, or even the opinions of friends and family. As a result, individuals often forfeit their individuality, losing sight of their own personal principles of existence that make us all human such as self-preservation in favor of conforming to what others deem acceptable , right for us , or successful.

Reclaiming one's mental, emotional, and spiritual well-being involves a conscious effort to break free from these external constraints. It begins with self-awareness—recognizing the ways in which external influences have shaped one's identity and decision-making processes that have led to the counterproductive choices we've against self. This involves reflecting on personal beliefs and values, distinguishing them from those imposed by society. Finding the right minds , right reading materials and engaging in deep conversations can facilitate this introspection.

Once individuals identify these influences along with the hurtful, disappointing, and unfair positions they've caused ,the next step is to set boundaries that will eliminate the reoccurrence of others being able to influence us, deceive us, or treat us in a negative way . This might mean reducing time spent with toxic relationships or limiting exposure to negative conversations.

By creating a safe space for personal growth, individuals can awaken and nurture their genuine selves back into existence, allowing their unique voices and passions to emerge.

Practicing self-compassion is essential in this journey. It encourages individuals to forgive themselves for past decisions made under external pressure and to embrace their imperfections with a new drive to improve those imperfections.

Engaging in activities that promote joy, creativity, and mindfulness can further reinforce this reclamation process.

Ultimately, reclaiming one's mental, emotional, and spiritual well-being is not just about personal empowerment; it is an act of courage.

By prioritizing your own needs and desires, you can forge a clearer sense of direction and purpose, leading to a more fulfilling life that honors your true selves. This journey fosters not only personal growth but also inspires others to embark on their own paths of self-discovery.

An individual's innate desire for love, comfort, and companionship can sometimes create vulnerabilities that emotional predators exploit.

In seeking connection, many individuals overlook red flags or fail to establish clear boundaries, driven by a longing for validation and acceptance.

This emotional instability often blurs the line between genuine relationships and manipulative ones with the greater potential to cause hurt and emotional suffering leading to blind trust in those who may not have proven their sincerity, good intentions, or ability to truly provide the loyalty , love, and respect that is sought after.

The quest for companionship can cloud judgment, causing individuals to prioritize the immediate gratification of connection over their long-term well-being.

Most people are prone to mistake or equate spending time together as a sign of love and caring. As a result, they may engage with people who present themselves favorably, yet lack the qualities essential for a supportive and healthy relationship.

This lack of clarity about one's best interests can lead to significant emotional harm, as the trust placed in these individuals is often unreciprocated and never justified.

To eliminate this risk, it is crucial for individuals to cultivate self-awareness and discernment. Establishing criteria for meaningful connections and allowing time for trust to build can help protect against emotional exploitation. By prioritizing self-love and clarity in their desires, individuals can create healthier relationships that enrich their lives rather than diminish them.

Truly Knowing and Understanding Yourself

The journey of knowing and understanding oneself is central to any meaningful pursuit in life. It is a foundational principle that echoes through various philosophies and spiritual teachings.

At its core, the principle that "everything else in life is an extension of self" positions self-awareness as not only a personal necessity but as a lens through which the external world must be engaged.

The importance of self-understanding lies in its ability to shape perception, guide decisions, and influence one's interactions with others and the world. Without it, the individual becomes disconnected from their own experiences, thereby leading to a fragmented existence.

First, self-awareness provides the framework for interpreting external experiences.
Everything we see, hear, and feel is processed through our consciousness. Therefore, how we react to events, people, and circumstances is directly linked to our internal thoughts, beliefs, values, and perceptions of ourselves.

For example, an individual with a strong sense of self-worth is likely to approach challenges with resilience and optimism, whereas someone who lacks this internal confidence may experience the same situation as overwhelming or disheartening. This disparity in interpretation underlines the argument that the external world is merely a reflection of the internal.

What we experience is deeply colored by how we see ourselves.

In addition, understanding oneself cultivates emotional intelligence, which is crucial for forming healthy relationships and achieving personal goals.

To navigate the complexity of human interactions, it's necessary to know and understand what drives us—our fears, desires, and motivations.

For example, in broken relationships, it is often not just external factors that lead to dissolution but internal misunderstandings, insecurities, and unaddressed personal issues.

Only when an individual is aware of their emotional triggers and psychological patterns can they create genuine connections with others, devoid of projections or unnecessary conflict. In this sense, knowing oneself serves as the foundation for authentic relationships, both romantic and platonic.

Furthermore, knowing oneself allows for a deeper connection to one's purpose in life. Life is filled with external noise—cultural expectations, societal pressures, and distractions that can easily divert an individual from their true path.

However, those who possess a strong sense of self are more likely to live with intentionality. Their choices—whether related to career, personal development, or spirituality—become extensions of their internal convictions rather than reactions to external pressures.

The alignment between self and external actions fosters a sense of fulfillment and meaning, as each decision is rooted in personal authenticity.

Another critical aspect of self-understanding is its role in overcoming personal limitations and mind locks, which are psychological barriers that restrict growth and prevent individuals from realizing their full potential. These limitations are often imposed by external institutions or internalized belief systems that condition individuals to think or act in specific ways.

However, when one is deeply attuned to their true nature, it becomes easier to identify these constraints and challenge them. By breaking free of imposed limitations, individuals can reclaim their autonomy and make empowered choices that reflect their true desires and capabilities.

Furthermore, the notion that "everything else in life is an extension of self" encourages reflection on the deeper aspects of life and the interconnectedness between us, all things outside of ourselves, and how we think ,believe, and feel from a foundation of self-awareness determines the quality of how well we become masters of our own destiny in our external environment.

When one understands themselves deeply, they realize that their actions, thoughts, and emotions do not exist in isolation. Instead, they ripple out and affect the world around them.

For instance, how one treats others is often a reflection of how they view themselves. A person who is compassionate and forgiving to themselves will likely extend the same grace to others.

In contrast, individuals plagued by self-loathing or unresolved guilt may project those feelings onto the people they encounter. This interconnectedness suggests that by knowing oneself, one can positively influence the external world, making it an extension of their inner peace and understanding.

In conclusion, the importance of knowing and understanding oneself cannot be overstated. It is the key to interpreting external experiences, building meaningful relationships, aligning with one's purpose, and breaking free from limitations.

In a world filled with distractions , others' harmful intentions, and external pressures, the individual's internal compass becomes the only true guide.

Therefore, self-awareness is not merely a personal luxury but a necessity for living an authentic and fulfilled life. All aspects of existence—from the relationships we form to the decisions we make—are merely extensions of the self. To know oneself is to know the world.

Individuals who are disconnected from themselves are often more likely to leave essential aspects of life to chance because they lack the internal clarity needed to make intentional, well-informed decisions.

When people do not understand their own desires, motivations, and emotional states, they are less equipped to plan and act with purpose. Instead, they may drift through life, allowing circumstances, external pressures, or the influence of others to shape and direct their path, rather than consciously directing their own actions.

Self-awareness is the foundation upon which purposeful planning and decision-making are built. When an individual knows themselves, they can set goals that align with their true values, strengths, and aspirations.

However, without this inner knowledge, life becomes more reactive than proactive.

A person disconnected from themselves may make impulsive decisions or avoid important life choices altogether, hoping that things will work out on their own.

This reliance on chance reflects a deeper uncertainty about who they are and what they truly want, leaving them vulnerable to external forces of influence that may not have their best interests at heart and unplanned outcomes that either initiate or increase dissatisfaction ,the sense of being unfulfilled, constantly confused, or lost.

For example, someone disconnected from their emotional needs may enter relationships without understanding what they truly seek in a partner. As a result, they might end up in unfulfilling or even toxic dynamics of their own making without realizing it, because they haven't taken the time to reflect on or discover what things actually mean in their true and fullest extent nor what's truly important to them.

Similarly, in career decisions, individuals who don't have a clear sense of their strengths or passions may follow the path of least resistance, accepting jobs or roles without considering if they align with their long-term goals or personal fulfillment.

In contrast, individuals who understand themselves are more intentional. They make plans rooted in self-knowledge and realistical facts that allows them to approach life's important factors—such as relationships, career, and personal growth—with a sense of purpose and clarity.

By knowing themselves, they take control, reducing the randomness in their lives and ensuring their actions are based on informed decisions rather than chance and personal uninformed assumptions.

Our negative and dysfunctional choices and behaviors often stem from a lack of self-knowledge and understanding.

When individuals do not fully comprehend their inner workings—their emotions, motivations, and subconscious patterns—they are more likely to act in ways that are destructive or self-sabotaging. These choices are not random but are reflections of unresolved internal conflicts, insecurities, a lack of truly knowing and understanding about something or unmet needs that remain hidden beneath the surface.

At the root of many dysfunctional behaviors is a disconnection from self.

Without self-awareness, people often act reactively, responding to external situations based on fear, anger, assumption, and past traumas, rather than thoughtful consideration and actual factual information.

For example, someone with low self-esteem may consistently make choices that undermine their well-being, such as staying in unhealthy relationships or engaging in self-destructive habits.

These behaviors are manifestations of their internal lack of self-worth, which they may not consciously understand. In this sense, their external choices mirror their internal confusion and unresolved emotional pain.

Furthermore, when individuals don't know themselves, they may also fall prey to societal pressures or external influences, leading them to make choices that do not align with their true values or desires.

This disconnect can result in feelings of dissatisfaction, frustration, or even resentment, which may drive them to act out in negative or dysfunctional ways. For instance, engaging in harmful behaviors, such as addiction or aggression, may serve as a coping mechanism for avoiding the deeper work of understanding and addressing internal struggles.

Ultimately, self-knowledge allows individuals to recognize their triggers, patterns, and emotional responses, enabling them to break the cycle of negative behaviors. By understanding themselves, people can make more conscious, aligned decisions that reflect their true needs and aspirations.

In contrast, a lack of self-awareness perpetuates dysfunctional choices, trapping individuals in patterns that only further distance them from living authentically and meaningfully.

Self-Revitalization Through Self-Realization

Contrary to the norm of the highly questionable and ineffective theories formulated by the field of psychology, there is major distinction between mere awareness of one's self and the realization of one's self.

Self-realization expresses a deeper sense of knowing and understanding one's own and others' thoughts, actions, and feelings and the deeper understanding of the motives and effects behind them.

This aspect is significant in the journey of self-discovery and emotional well-being. Awareness serves as the first step in recognizing what is happening internally and externally. It involves observing thoughts, feelings, and behaviors without judgment, allowing individuals to identify their immediate emotional states and reactions.

However, this level of awareness can often be superficial, focusing on surface-level experiences without delving into the underlying reasons that shape them.

Awareness signifies a superficial surface knowledge of things which precludes one from being able to broach the sphere of self where our natural talents and abilities reside.

Self-realization requires deeper, prolonged ,and more extensive thought and analyzation of things.

In contrast to awareness, realizing the deeper motives, nature and effects of things involves a more profound introspection. This entails exploring the "why" behind thoughts and actions, acknowledging past experiences, societal influences, and personal beliefs that form one's emotional landscape.

Understanding these deeper layers allows individuals to focus and connect their thoughts, feelings ,and behaviors to their core natural abilities, potentials and unmet needs, fostering a more comprehensive self-knowledge and understanding. It enables one to discern patterns, recognize triggers, and ultimately understand how these elements influence their interactions and emotional responses.

This deeper realization is crucial for reclaiming one's identity and emotional sanity. It empowers individuals to break free from reactive patterns and cultivate healthier responses aligned with their true selves.

When one comprehends the motives behind their feelings, it becomes possible to engage in meaningful self-reflection and growth. This not only enhances self-knowledge and self's performance but also improves relationships with others, fostering empathy and understanding.

Ultimately, the journey from mere awareness to the deeper understandings that only self-realization can offer and secure is transformative, paving the way for emotional resilience and a more genuine and fortified existence.

In our surroundings, many individuals find themselves ensnared in a web of expectations imposed by others. These expectations often stem from family, peers, societal norms, and cultural standards, leading to a self-imposed detrimental position where people prioritize the external validation of others over their own sense of self.

Going further, the relentless pursuit of conforming to others', ideas, beliefs, expectations can significantly hinder self-realization and personal growth.

When individuals measure their own worth or sense of direction based on how well they meet external expectations, that is the most crucial point when people actually begin to lose themselves and their own natural abilities ,potentials, power of thinking, and aspirations. This can manifest in various areas of life, including career choices, personal relationships, and even lifestyle decisions. For instance, a person may choose a career path that pleases their parents or fits societal norms, rather than pursuing what truly inspires or fulfills them. As a result, they may find themselves trapped in roles that do not resonate with their genuine natural selves, leading to dissatisfaction and a sense of emptiness.

Sadly, the pressure to conform can foster a constant cycle of comparison.

Individuals often look to others as a measuring standard for success, adopting behaviors, beliefs, and goals that align with those they admire or feel pressured to emulate. This imitation can create a false sense of success, masking the underlying discontent that arises from not being true to oneself.

The more one tries to fit into the mold created by others, the further one drifts away from their unique identity and the things that naturally support and nurture their own individuality.

This manifestation of the disconnect from self-realization can lead to feelings of anxiety, inadequacy, and even depression, as individuals struggle to reconcile their true selves with the personality and functions they project to the world.

Compounding this issue is the prevalence of movies, television, and social media, where artificially constructed images, roles, and stories amplify feelings of inadequacy and pressure to conform.

People often compare their unfiltered lives to the highlight reels of others, reinforcing the belief that they must change themselves to fit a particular ideal. This external focus stifles introspection, self-discovery, self-improvement, and self-preservation further perpetuating the cycle of seeking approval rather than producing and fostering a genuinely strong foundation of self-realization.

Breaking free from this cycle requires a conscious effort to prioritize self-discovery and being authentic with and towards one's self. It involves questioning the ideas, beliefs, and standards imposed by others and reflecting on personal values, desires, and goals.

Individuals must learn to embrace their unique identities, understanding that true fulfillment comes not from conforming to external expectations but from honoring and valuing one's individuality.

By fostering self-realization, individuals can cultivate a more profound sense of purpose, inner stability, and confidence, empowering them to approach and overcome life's challenges on their own terms.

Ultimately, reclaiming one's identity is essential for personal growth and a meaningful existence, allowing individuals to thrive and advance rather than merely just trying to survive in a world filled with external pressures and influences that seek to dissuade, hinder, and shatter one's individuality.

Self-realization is the in-depth and profound understanding of oneself, encompassing one's foundation of thinking, values, strengths, weaknesses, and purpose in life.

This awareness plays a critical role in determining an individual's success or failure. When we achieve self-realization, we unlock the most powerful part of ourselves and the most powerful potential within ourselves that influences our decision-making processes and how we approach life's choices and challenges.

Individuals who possess a strong sense of self-realization are often more capable of identifying their own skills and talents.

This recognition allows them to leverage their strengths when facing obstacles, leading to more effective problem-solving.

For example, an individual who understands their ability to communicate well may be more inclined to seek collaboration or help when confronted with a challenge, thereby expanding their resource pool.

This proactive approach not only enhances their ability to overcome difficulties with a high rate of efficiency and sufficiency but also fosters a high degree of resilience, enabling them to bounce back from setbacks.

Consequently, the lack of self-realization can severely limit one's perspective.

When individuals are unaware of their potentials and capabilities, they may find themselves trapped in a cycle of self-doubt and indecision. This can lead to a narrow view of available options, causing them to feel overwhelmed by life's challenges.

A prime example is, someone who does not recognize their organizational skills may struggle to manage time effectively during a stressful project, leading to decreased performance and increased anxiety.

The inability to see beyond one's limitations can create a self-fulfilling prophecy, where the lack of belief in oneself directly contributes to failure.

Furthermore, self-realization is intrinsically linked to the number of options available for problem-solving. Awareness of one's strengths often correlates with a broader perspective in addressing issues.

In contrast, individuals with limited self-awareness may resort to familiar but ineffective ideas, beliefs, and strategies that restrict their ability to innovate or adapt. This can lead to a stagnation in personal growth, as they may consistently shy away from challenges that require stepping outside their comfort zone.

To summarize it all, self-realization serves as a key determinant in our successes and failures. It empowers individuals to recognize their capabilities and expand their problem-solving options, fostering resilience and adaptability.

On the other hand, a lack of self-realization's confines individuals to a limited viewpoint and ultimately a limited base of potential and power from which to act, thus hindering their ability to effectively tackle life's difficulties.

It can't be expressed or emphasized enough that cultivating self-realization is essential for personal and professional growth, enabling us to meet and overcome challenges with confidence, trust in the sufficiency of our own abilities, and creativity in the times of difficulties or crisis.

CHAPTER 7

Acquiring The Power To Identify, Understand & Remedy The Source Of The Dysfunctions

How is it that someone can claim to love someone else but cause so much pain, disappointment, and sadness in their lives?

How is it that the majority of the world's people claim to know and understand love or claim to be loving others in friendships, relationships, family and marriages but only end up causing that which is negative, hurtful, trifling, and destructive?

How is it that the prevalence of those negative elements are so widely spread throughout EVERY city of EVERY nation until love seems non-existent except in a few isolated examples?

A few isolated examples themselves that have proven to seem one way on the surface but turned out to be something totally different underneath the surface.

A very significant example is numerous 80 + year old couples having been married 50 + years but didn't have a clue about love but considered love to be caring, companionship, and compromise etc.

The most alarming fact about it was , none of them could in the least amount define or explain what it was that they bv were calling love. Thereby revealing a central fear of loneliness and a acute fear of being without companionship as the main reason that bonded them together for so long thus not love.

The answers to these seemingly vast problems and dysfunctions have confounded many of the academic world for centuries mainly because they tried to understand and define a natural thing and a natural process by artificial standards and the outer appearance rather than the internal where the essence of all things exists.

This explains clearly the part that the world of academics has played in adding to the dysfunctions.

Not surprisingly, the origins of the modern academic understanding of the human being and human nature was limited or distorted by theologies with no basis in fact.

The basis of what the world has assumed was love originates from the Eurocentric Greek Fathers of Greek philosophy and other Greek Philosophy.

The same Greek

Father's of Philosophy and the same Greek philosophy that proved to be nothing more than hypothetical and theorized teachings full of ideas about the existence of things that they nor the level of Greek Civilization's technical science could prove the existence of or provide a confirmable model for.

The Greeks had 6 to 8 words for love and neither one of them and the defini8or Philosophy attached to them ever revealed what love exactly was in and of itself.

1. **Agape** – Love for family, spouse, children, etc. (Modern Christians try to interpret this ” Agape “ as meaning "Unconditional Love" but there is no factual basis for that misinterpretation because there was no Greek word signifying (Unconditionally) ever attached to it and how the Greeks during the time of the great philosophers interpreted "Agape".

2. **Eros** – Romantic Love

3. **Philia** – Affectionate Love

4. **Storge** – Familiar Love

5. **Mania** – Obsessive Love

6. **Ludus** – Playful Love

7. **Pragma** – Enduring Love

8. **Philautia** – Self Love

Just as there are physical laws of nature such as gravity that dictate the realm of human potential and possibility, likewise there exists laws of thinking and behavior that dictate the realm of human potential, possibility, and impossibility. What one will experience or won't experience.

All of which is directly relative to love, the dysfunctions that prevent the facilitation of love, the remedying of those dysfunctions, and the actual nature of love itself. A nature that exists outside of the boundaries of what a foolish world has tried to define it as.

It may come as a surprise to learn that we as humans are subject to laws of existence that are beyond our control and are the most influential and determining factors of who we are, what we think ,and what we do no matter how much we may deceive or fool ourselves to think, feel, and believe otherwise.

It is that exact self- delusionment that also lies at the very heart of all dysfunctions in human relations.

The prime example of these (Laws of existence) is one that exists as an unavoidable prerequisite to all that we could ever think or do. So much so until it even determines whether one will even be allowed (to begin) to realize love or not, whether one will or won't come to know and understand love and whether one will or won't come to experience the full capacity of love.

"The Nature by which we approach a thing, directly dictates the nature of the results received. "

That being expressed is proven by our approach to love in all of its numerous forms and degrees of intensity and power. An approach that in of itself actually creates the dysfunctions in human relations (friendships, family, relationships, and marriages).

The nature of those approaches are best formulated and measured by the following scale.

- **Improper Fraction Of Perception : Seeing Is knowing & Understanding Love.**

- **Individualized Love**

- **The Need To Be In Control: Its bitter & Poisonous Fruits Of Preferences and Conditional Intent**

- **The Standard Communication Process: A Symbol Without Substance**

Improper Fraction Of Perception: Seeing Is Knowing & Understanding Love

When it comes to our initial approach to things in life, it is our faculty of sight that primarily acquaints us with something, and the matter of love is no different in that regard.

Our first impressions of love , even from a very young age , is based upon our observation of the various interactions between male and females, with certain actions, holding hands, hugging, spending time together, or even kissing.

That particular stage is very significant because it is an initial stage of growth that carries on into our older age groups of young adult and adulthood with a primary perception and understanding of love based upon what we have observed.

Unknowingly, this places us in a situation that is comparable to the situation of an adolescent boy or girl seeing older children riding bicycles where just by the mere fact of the child seeing the act of riding a bicycle, he or she immediately believe they can do it. Feelings then come in and deepen the premature thinking that it's easy and simple enough as just merely getting on the bicycle and copying what was seen but then the critical moment arrives when the adolescent boy or girl gets on the bicycle only to experience fall after fall.

Experience then brings the child into a fuller reality about bicycle riding that their level of observation didn't and couldn't reveal to them or prepare
them for.

That necessary element of the acquisition of balance and coordination upon a bicycle that could only be developed through practice and experience.

What was the result ? It was a hard and painful lesson learned that taught the adolescent child that observing and trying to copy other's actions and just simply getting on a bicycle wasn't a complete thing in and of itself but was actually just stages in a process that involved other necessary elements before riding the bicycle could even be possible.

What is the point of that bicycle analogy?

It is basically symbolic but highly relevant to the human approach to love that has barred the human & our human experiences from actually consisting of love and being able to bring love into an actual reality within our lives and the world.

Why? How? Because love isn't some external object or external event that one can observe, measure, nor understand and perform from the basis of a seen interaction between material objects in material circumstances outside of the human.

Why or how is that so? because love exists an internal force of positive power and influence whose exact state or condition (basically it's form) is undetectable by the human eye and ultimately is only available and approachable through a process of introspection that love itself generates and compels within the one in whom love has become awakened.

This is a position that is naturally going to make some people very uncomfortable because it takes away one of the main senses that we humans use to analyze and measure things in our external environment. This position in reality is not a bad position at all, it's a position that will force us to become more acquainted with the principle internal vision of the heart and mind .0

Love and one of the primary significant elements of its nature's function is to emanate from within one person's mind and heart in an outward direction towards another or others so that it can connect with another part of itself in others and become a greater degree of itself in expression, power, and influence beyond the limited but highly necessary singular existence within just one person for the purpose of establishing self love in that person.

A love for self that exists in moderation, never to the extreme because only in moderation can that love have the ability and power to truly interact with others and connect with them from one of love's main defining directives that love compels one to naturally think and act from.

".....love the next person as one loves self "

because love doesn't discriminate, it recognizes itself in ALL persons whether it has become awakened in them or not and facilitates the truth, purity ,goodness, and fairness of its nature towards all according to another defining element of its nature's function, (Unconditionally) so that it may in time influence its existence in others to become awakened.

Seeing with the physical eyes and initially basing everything upon that is a stage of learning and perception that is natural when it comes to our learning experiences.

It is through our learning experiences that we come into the realization of a proper and improper process of learning about how to truly learn to know and understand things.

Initially, our very first experiences should teach us at an early age that what we see and observe is never the complete picture or complete knowledge and understanding of a thing's nature and true existence.

That is a lesson that very few of us have learned and as a serious consequence, this is where the initial beginning of the dysfunctions in human relations began and continues to originate from.

It is through the mentality of "Seeing is knowing and understanding" that has caused us to improperly perceive the role that our eyes play in actual knowledge and understanding of love.

Instead of properly perceiving sight and observation in its proper context of only being a very minute element, we've made it the most significant element that determines what love is.

The decision to place sight, actions, and external events and their external circumstances in the primary position has as a consequence produced the means by which we would be missing love altogether.

Why? Or How? because this fixation on what our eyes can see and observe has in an unnatural way made perceivable actions the primary defining factor of what love is to us and has also made the outer materialistic part of things the total and complete manifestation of what love is us as well.

In truth and fact, the physically observed actions are only a small secondary link in the expression and functions of love.

Contrary to what people have heard or been deceived and influenced to think, love isn't an action but manifests a portion of its intent through actions, where actions represent physical indicators that love may be present but not necessarily present, Because there are emotions and desires that can influence the exact same actions as caring, companionship, and tenderness but have
nothing to do with love.

How so ? because the actions that originate from love bear a totally different nature, lifespan, and purpose that is always unconditional, consistent ,and supremely enduring of all situations, circumstances, and time periods, thereby being contrary to all that we as humans have constructed and defined as love, that has always been momentarily, limited, inconsistent, and highly conditioned upon other things of a trifling, insignificant, and selfish nature.

The imbalanced and immature mind is always grounded upon the superficial aspects of external things of a physical nature.

Sadly, that is where we then miss the internal things of the heart, and love's internal and eternal place of existence that the eyes can't observe.

In light of that, it shouldn't come as a surprise to learn that that is the exclusive reason why the world's views and assumptions about love naturally positions all things and all relations that are based upon it into the unavoidable position of always being predetermined to fail.

Why is that position naturally inclined towards failure ? Because as the external things and situations it is based upon are always changing , this as a consequence disrupts the original form and position of what was liked and repositions such things into being undesirable so that they no longer hold any attractiveness, and just simply outlived their purpose. Although a trifling purpose.

Don't get the wrong understanding here.This isn't just about what you call romantic love.

This also applies equally to the love that we as humans call ourselves demonstrating in our family structures.

Our past observations and experiences with family love were based primarily upon our observations and experiences with various situations that we were either apart of or observed others engaged in which formed a reference point of what to do or not to do and how to think or how not to think in regards to certain situations and events that occurred in the family.

This very reference frame for thought and actions within the family structure is the number one reason and origin for child abuse, child neglect, gangs, teenage runaways, and foster children.

How so? because that so-called family love was expressed continuously but always manifested itself as being something totally different.

Prime example:

"I love you" but actions showed that :

"My fear of something or someone is greater than my love for you"

You might wonder how this could ever be a realistic situation involving that principle of thought.

Imagine a parent or parents , grandparents, or aunts and uncles who have called the police on a child or teenager under their guardianship and reported them to the police as having either committed a crime or about to commit a crime.

What kind of family would do such a thing? Its one thing not to condone bad behavior or illegal activities but its something totally different when a so-called family member will be the cause of another family member going to jail or prison because they disagreed with the family member's activities and valued or feared man's laws more than they loved their own flesh and blood.

Laws by a particular kind of man (Caucasian) who have NEVER applied any of their laws equally to Blacks or other people of color.

"I love you" but actions showed : **" My want of a girlfriend or boyfriend is greater than my love for you"**

"I love you" but actions showed that : "My hatred for what you do or how you think is greater than my love for you ... .so get out of my house".

There are certain situations where a parent or guardian must remove a family member from their home because of a security risk they may pose to the home like it being targeted for a shooting.

Surprisingly,   there are innumerable incidents where teenagers or young adults are being forced out the home just simply because they refuse to think and behave like the authority figures in the home.

"I love you" but actions showed : **"you're in trouble with the law so deal with it on your own... no letters from me, visits, or support but once you're out of jail or prison, I will love you again"**

What kind of real and true family member does this?

What kind of real and true friends do this?

Obviously, this is the basis of what is now called being the natural way that family and friends treat people they claim to have love for.

As the course of time moves on, there has been a rapid deterioration of the values and standards of what a family and friend are composed of and it's only going to worsen.

 or even

"I love you" but actions showed : **" You're only as valuable as what i can get from you"**

" I love you " but actions showed: **" If you can't and won't be like me and**

 do as I say, then I don't want to deal with you"

Or within friendships...

" I love you" but actions showed : **"We can't be friends unless you agree with me or like what I like"**

This kind of artificial love exists because of what people saw and observed being done towards others as children in a family structure or being done by society or even saw and observed being done towards them as children by the family structure or society which naturally transferred into adulthood as a reference frame of how to think and act within a family or friendship, or relationship structure thus continuing the cycle of dysfunction in the name of love.

The proliferation of the world's dysfunctional human relations lies heavily at the feet of the academic world that is not only educational universities with psychology but are also facilities of learning that seeks to define or influence human thought and beliefs thus religious institutions as well that have been influenced primarily by man under the disguises of The Creator's names.

Psychology and the majority of man's religious teachings have historically taught and still currently teach that love is an emotion or feeling.

All of the things that are classified as emotions and feelings such as anger, disappointment, fear, happiness, and loneliness are essentially defined as reactions to things (Situations, Circumstances, people, physical objects etc.) external to one's self.

Love isn't a reaction to anything so if love is just an emotion or feeling as the so-called experts say and teach, then why and how is it that love is capable of overpowering ALL other emotions, setting boundaries and restrictions for ALL emotions and feelings that they can not overcome? Why and how is that love can even cause all emotions and feelings that are not conducive to its purpose to become voided?

That indisputably infers and solidifies the fact that love's ultimate nature is significantly different from the emotions and feelings that it has been classified with.

The answer is not only very refreshing and enlivening but is indomitable as well.

Love is not an emotion or feeling although it facilitates both in the process of making itself known to the one or ones in whom it has become awakened.

Indivindividualized Love

When it comes to people in the world being asked about love the response that one usually gets is that they have their own particular idea and opinion about what love is.

The thought never occurs whether anyone else can relate to it or not or whether how it can cause negative and detrimental effects towards others.

Most people do not see anything wrong with this particular perception because they feel like love is something that they should be able to define based upon their own individual experiences.

No one perceives this particular position as being wrong in any way.

Why? because people want to believe that love is under their control and that they have a right to direct their love towards whom and whatever they choose like "love interests" to the exclusion of anything else or a family to the exclusion of everything else.

This is a very significant perception that most people in the world have about love that stems from ignorance and selfishness. This
belief that we as individuals can define and direct our love in any way that best suits us as individuals and places everything beyond our individuality as a nonessential to love is actually the catalyst through which numerous dysfunctions are produced.

The idea of one even thinking of this individualized love as being a dysfunction and as well creating dysfunction is something that is bound to make someone very uncomfortable and highly in disagreeable out of the feeling of someone attempting to wrestle something from them that they have an exclusive right to conceive and implement in any manner that they so choose.

It has been said that there are nine wonders of the world that cause awe and wonderment but one of the most highly underrated wonders of the world that should be added into that category is ,how is it that individuals can think, feel and believe that they can conceive of things with their own definitions and ideas
about a particular thing that has no basis in reality or nature and then wonder why it is so hard and impossible for others to connect with it and receive anything positive and nurturing from it ?

This particular perception of individualized love in reality is not designed to be about others ,it's not designed to include the feelings ,wants, desires or needs of others. It possesses no true or genuine position in regards to others at all , it is all about an individual.

There is a widely spread assumption that one can have their very own perception and understanding about love, although true in one minor way, that is totally false and wrong in all of the most significant and most defining ways about love.

How so? love brings its own standards ,definitions ,and reasons to the table of Human Experience where although it manifests itself to and within different individuals, every manifestation has the same basic Foundation ,nature, intent ,aim ,purpose and Direction within the
different contexts of different people's lives so that all of the different people can be unified or connected on the same page of love with the same positive nurturing principles involved.

There are approximately close to 5 billion people in the world and the problem comes about with the idea, belief and perception of one being able to have a personal individualized love that is exclusively defined by them.

When you have close to five billion people with five billion different ideas, opinions, and feelings about love ,what you naturally end up with is the current state of the world ,massive dysfunctions in human relations where almost five billion different ideas and opinions about love that conflict with each other, have no common aims, purposes, directions or meaning. So much so until these almost five billion different ideas and opinions about love cause nothing but conflict, confusion, chaos, pain ,hurt ,and misunderstanding in the Name of Love.

What are the origins of the idea of there being such a thing as an individualized love?

No one who thinks and feels such away about love has ever asked themselves the question of what makes them better qualified to define love better than love itself?

In our immature mentality and expressions of human nature we act as though love came into this world the moment we as an individual came to exist.

There are numerous reasons as to why a person would want an individualized version of love but two of the main reasons are that no one likes to be in a position of having to admit they just don't know something about a very significant thing due to an exaggerated fear of being positioned as powerless, stupid, or unworthy and incapable of having something or someone desired.

No matter the actual amount of the reasons available to explain this individualized love , all of them have a common nature that derives from selfishness and ignorance taken to its extreme point.

As with any dysfunction, the basic definition of dysfunction is the inability of a person ,place ,thing, or idea to function in the way it was designed or intended.

With all of that being said, what is presented to us is a unique position that is bound to make us initially uncomfortable but within that position lies the central remedy to any dysfunction.

That position is in fact a question that we must ask ourselves and depending upon how honest we are willing to be with ourselves ,we will either open the door to finally being able to fix our dysfunctions or we will continue to lie to ourselves and continue to produce the exact impediments that are causing the dysfunctions in human relations in the name of love.

That very question is, did you yourself create or originate love? If you realize that you didn't ,then your answer at the same time must be allowed to reposition your thinking into realizing and understanding that there exists a predetermined model and standard of what love is, that must be conformed to rather than us in our warped and immature thinking believing that we as individuals must always distort or force everything around us to conform to us as an individual and our individual limitations and defects.

In reality this whole idea, opinion, and theory about individualized love is to a greater extent about the kind of individual and the individual desires that individuals like to disguise under nice and shiny names like love so that ulterior motives and intentions can attract other people to them so that they can receive some form of benefit at the expense of others kindness, sincerity, and dignity. That can be money, financial security, sex,social status, or even just plain old influence and control over another.

Okay I understand that presents another major problem of (you) not knowing where to find that predetermined model or standard of love because this world hasn't produced it, although they would like us to think, believe, and feel otherwise. But you'll find it here.

The Need To Be In Control : Its Bitter & Poisonous Fruits Of Preferences & Conditional Intent

This desire or compulsion of needing to be in control in part stems from a mentality saturated with impatience, frustration and an overwhelming feeling of wanting what one wants in an instant. It's comparable to instant microwave popcorn or dinners with the thought "Oh I'll just put this prepackaged love in the microwave and I'll have it instantly with a minimum wait and no risk factor."

The control Factor says "It's My Life ,my wants ,so I'll determine the time it needs and when it's ready regardless of any instructions involved"

Sadly, this very thought process isn't about popcorn, this is the main idea that the world has in reference to being able to ultimately control love.

Everywhere you go in this world ,one of the main first things you'll hear people say when it comes to them seeking a relationship or Love is "I'm looking for that which is drama free" not realizing that in a world built upon being Loveless, the moment you find true love the world is going to bring you drama up close and personal in constant streams to test it and to tear it apart. Tests that more than often involve a problem that makes one or both involved very uncomfortable, frustrated, or depressed.

This is the critical moment when those who feel the need to be in control react with the usual response to such. "This isn't what I was looking for"

That is the strange and sometimes funny thing about life in this world when it comes to people and the things that they believe that they want. When it comes to most things that people believe they want ,usually they're only looking at maybe one or two particular things while excluding the existence of other things that naturally exist with the particular thing they believe they want.

Naturally when they reach a point in dealing with that thing that they say they wanted, they discover that there are other elements there that actually pose particular contrary actions, thoughts, and experiences that they didn't want and wasn't ready for, then they say "oh this isn't really what I wanted"

Most times this type of

situation will always be blamed on others as something bad or negative that others did to them when in fact, the blame always rests upon the one who assumed that a particular thing is naturally only one sided or one dimensional in the way they wanted it to be. It's a hard truth to face but it's their own limited immature thoughts and desires that blinded them to the complete reality of what they thought they were wanting.

The need to be in control, a widespread aspect of human behavior, leads to significant imbalances in personal and professional relationships.

The desire for control derives from an acute fear of uncertainty and an exaggerated desire for predictability.

In personal relationships, such as those between partners, friends, or family members, the drive to control can manifest itself in the form of attempted dominance, manipulation, or coercion which results in an imbalance within all relations that such a mentality becomes involved in.

Whenever there exists one individual or groups of alike individuals who consistently seeks to enforce their will, it undermines and destroys any potential for respect, empathy, fairness, trust and equality to exist which are necessary essentials for healthy interactions.

The inevitable result
 of this dynamic is the production of resentment, the erosion of trust and genuine communication, and the loss of any moral compass which to most individuals who seek to be in control, doesn't even matter because when all is said and done, it's all about what they want, how they want it, where they want it, how much and how long they want it without regard for who gets hurt, used, or deprived unfairly as a result of it.

When it comes to the subject of love, this approach of needing to be in control manifests itself in numerous forms.

It derives from a delusional mentality that an individual in of themselves can dictate meaning, purpose, and function to all things in life dealing with it or surrounding it.

That particular method and mentality usually produces good consistent results when dealing with material things and material based situations such as jobs, careers, hobbies, and sports because they are all the product of human thought and planning but have not , do not, and will not produce the good or right results when it comes to love.

The need to be in control, while often felt to be a strength, can lead to significant personal negative and counterproductive ramifications.

Control is perceived as the only means by which a sense of order and predictability can be established in their lives, enabling individuals to control or restrict life's uncertainties with confidence.

At its core, the desire for control stems from a basic human need for security and stability. When individuals feel in control, they believe they can prevent undesirable outcomes and dictate control over their lives.

When it comes to love the need to be in control manifest itself in the form of such thoughts as :

"I don't want to be heartbroken or deceived so I'll confine my idea of love to certain areas and only deal with certain types of people who are more susceptible to what I want and how I want it without regard for themselves "

"I am willing to consider a person a possible love interest only if they can fit within the confinements of my lifestyle "

" Love is defined by me as something that won't challenge or disrupt what i think is best for myself and the way I want my life to reflect only what I consider to be valuable and comforting. "

"Love isn't a reaction to anything external "

This can lead to a crucial paradox where the pursuit of control becomes a source of stress and tension not only to the individual seeking control but to those who have to deal with the controlling individual because there persists a constant striving to control every aspect of one's environment which also in a major way involves the relentless attempt to control other people and the interactions. It is the unpredictability of life that inevitably disrupts these efforts.

Furthermore, the need to be in control negatively impacts all relations with others.

People who exhibit controlling behaviors often seek to impose their will, desires ,expectations and standards on others which always leads to conflicts and resentment. This can result in a cycle of misunderstandings and emotional distance.

In addition to interpersonal issues, the need to be in control hinders personal growth.

Embracing the uncertainty factor of life is a crucial component of learning and development. When individuals seek to control their experiences within a small perimeter of their own making , they limit their exposure to new ideas and new opportunities.

With the individuals who feel a need to be in control, there's always the delusional idea that this position is in the best interests of themselves and others.

Preferences

We as people are by Nature beings who initially perceive and interpret everything about ourselves and around us according to the senses (sight, taste,touch,smell, hearing, and sound).

As we grow mentally through our experiences with the physical surroundings a Form of Intelligence should have been developed in the mind that suggests and compels us to know and understand that living things are defined more precisely and correctly by the inner substance of their minds which will reveal their very nature and the realm of potential and definite situations that can or will occur in an experience with those things.

Contrary to that, 99.9% of people have developed an ignorant approach to the relations that are meant to provide us with love and as a consequence, it has become a highly common result to end up with that which is other than love.

That ignorant approach is the development of some sort of preference for particular facial and body features or financial situations or other similar external circumstances that a person has to possess in order to be considered possibly the right one for us, beautiful, hot ,handsome, desirable ,or suitable for ourselves in dating, relationships, and marriage.

The preferences themselves aren't ignorant, it's when these preferences are positioned as a prerequisite to love that defines this approach as ignorant and foolish.

How so? First and foremost this preference approach presupposes to dictate to love a set of Standards by which it would be willing to be open or susceptible to love but if these standards aren't present in a person, then they are concluded as being unacceptable and not even up for consideration.

The ignorant and selfish basis for these particular prefe7rences lies more often than anything up on the principle of a sexual attraction that arouses excitement within us upon seeing these particular individuals.

This sexual attraction is then taken out of context and turned into a warped standard of measurement that precedes to define not only the potential or lack of potential for an individual to possess the distorted version of love (that we have in mind) and is sought after by us but as well proceeds to define the ultimate worth of an individual by his or her material outer characteristics.

This is the particular distorted ,incorrect, and delusional ideas that people have formed in their minds and hearts about love in order to cheapen what Love Actually is, so that it presents no particular responsibility, meaning, or dictates to them in pursuing such shallow-minded things that they have designed and titled under the Name of Love.

These particular preferences are in and of themselves a unique status of insanity that are based upon an external perception and definition that seeks to disqualify any other particular significant element as a defining factor in what a particular thing is so that the nature, event and circumstances surrounding it all will become simplified and based upon an animalistic urge that incites the senses.

Such a one who is possessing these particular preferences acquires that which isn't lasting, stable, or consistent as love is, then they naturally assume that the problem is with other people rather than with themselves who initiated something that wasn't love and naturally received results that didn't have anything to do with love.

The insanity then deepens to the point of formulating the idea that if they change the locations, age groups, or social status of where they look for love, then the results will be different.

All along setting themselves up for the same results no matter what they change or restructure because they haven't changed the essence of their perceptions and approach which is those shallow minded preferences that believe the substance of love is to be found behind outer symbols as a set category of particular outer appearances.

Once again you cannot define an inner eternal process of a spiritual nature by the restraints and confinements of that which is physical and readily seen.

Whether you believe in spiritual or spirituality or not, the mind and the process involved with thinking is and shall forever be that which is composed of unseen positive energy that derives from a more powerful source than thought itself and that is a particular standard and rule of judgment that is based upon the definitions and principles of the ancient civilizations of the world.

Ancients who were more in sync with that which is called spiritual than modern people have ever been.

All of those ancient civilization's (non Greek, Crete, Roman) mystery schools of higher teachings equated spirit with mind and thinking, the particular feelings that derived from such thinking, an inner source of energy that rested as the source of the mind, that not only connected human beings at the very essence of who we are but also connected the essence of human beings to all things in the universe along with the effects that thinking was able to produce upon the external environment.

The most profound thing about this need to be in control is that it also invades and seeks to define a significant aspect within that which some people call their religious beliefs.

In the Biblical scriptures, it is said that "God is Love" but when it comes to love, most of those in the church or those who claim to believe in God and that biblical verse will tell you anything from their mouths about God being in control or how one must give God control but when you see them in action and listen to them outside of the church, what you discover is a total different reality.

A reality where even they are bound by having the same preferences and a overwhelming need to be in control of who they chose to love and how they chose to love which in reality says

" God is love but this is my life, my heart, and my right to choose something according to my own standards so I'll just put God over there in the corner with God's love because I can't sleep with God, kiss God, or be held by God".

Conditional Intent

"Conditional intent" is the most defining nature of the world's overall view, understanding, and application of what it falsely calls love.

This is probably the hardest fact that one has to face when it comes to what they call love or have been indirectly taught about how love works in the world.

When it comes to people loving others in this world, what you find is the majority of the people in the world who are always at some point in their life where they tell someone that they love them or are in love with them and on the surface this would seem to imply that this is a commitment of loyalty, respect ,and honor forever.

Time and time again it is realized that these are only mere words to people that people use to gain particular things that they desire or value for temporary moments in time.

What usually happens is that those words translate into contradictory words and actions that actually mean

"I love you as long as you think and act the way I want you to think and act"

" I want to be around you as long as you do those things that make me happy",

"I love you as long as you're willing to give me what I want or need"

, also two of the all time favorites,
"I love you as long as you have what I want"

and " I love you as long as you're near me"
which means that if a problem or difficulty arises that takes you away temporarily, then it's **"out of sight ,out of mind".**

This explains why the average friendship, marriage, and relationship never last because those who have entered into these particular relations have known deep in their heart and their minds that they have only entered into these particular relations with certain conditions attached to it , although they may lead others to believe otherwise.

This conditional intent as well applies to the dysfunctions in the family structure because the love that is supposed to be there naturally isn't there, what is found in its place is something that's masquerading as love and most of the times usually ends up being very hurtful, disrespectful, disloyal, dishonest, and uncommitted to the ones they are saying that they love within these particular family structures.

Sadly, it always boils down to something else being more valuable than the one that is said to be loved and this particular love is always applied with conditions.

It's like "as long as you do what we want you to do we will love you", "as long as you behave within the confinements that we have set for you we will love you" or as long as you pattern your life after our lives, standards, and expectations then we will love you but when you fail to do so and choose to be different ,we can no longer love you".

These are some of the most hurtful and destructive characteristics displayed in many families all across the world in the Name of Love.

Surprisingly, the conclusion is that most people who believe in love this way and demonstrate love this way actually find something wrong with the person that they demonstrated this particular perverted caricature of Love towards rather than finding something wrong with their application of what they considered to be love.

There is an ultimate truth when it comes to misunderstanding love and the dysfunctions that are produced from these misunderstandings and that ultimate truth actually involves another major element of the nature of real love.

Love acts unconditionally in a continuous flow towards the object of Love's Focus.

Loving someone and the facilitation of that love towards someone must always remain continuously and unconditionally regardless of what the object of our love does or thinks that is contrary to our particular expectations and standards.

Love is not blind , love is not ignorant ,love is not foolish but love exists and overcomes all of these particular things in its realest form.

Love doesn't mean that you have to accept anything from a family member that you disagree with.

What it does mean though when it comes to love and truly loving, if it is real, it will always outweigh that which is disliked about a particular family member and will come to exist even more stronger with the best of wishes and hopes for that particular family member as we love them enough to allow them to have to experience some things in life on their own that will teach them the lessons that mouths and words can't.

It may come as a surprise to many but even on their own, the love positions true family members to always make it known, "If you need us, we are always here with open arms".

Love doesn't prejudge no one because love knows that people must get their own experiences in life which means making their own mistakes but no human is ever beyond change or redemption and as long as a person lives, change is forever possible.

The Standard Communication Process: A Symbol Without Substance

It's a well voiced idea that communication is the key to solving misunderstanding, problems, and many other dysfunctions that plague Humanity's relations with each other.

That is true to a major limited extent and that is expressed as being so because when it comes to the human relations such as friendships, relationships, family, and marriage, what is more significant than just the communication process itself is the nature of the communication.

The substance of the communication, and the origins and nature of that substance to be instilled within the communication is the most determining element of it all.

When it comes to relationships and the presence of a dysfunction within it ,the first cliché that gets stated and repeated is "there's a breakdown in the communication process" but the hard hitting truth in that matter is that the reasons most relationships ,marriages friendships, and family structures fail is because there never was truly a real communication process established there from the beginning.

Therefore in reality, the thought or act of attempting to eliminate or heal the elements that are causing a breakdown in the communication process within the particular relation is more like trying to fix something that's never been there in the first place.

How can that be said and proven as a fact and truth? Quite easily.

Okay, from the very beginning of your relationship or relationship that evolved into marriage, what were the exact substances conveyed in the conversation between you and your so-called love interest? Was it not just simply favorite colors ,favorite foods, favorite movies, the revealing of each other's birthdays, each other's likes and dislikes, jokes, family background, each other's job status and job nature, what each wanted in life, fashion, Club, Church, each other's belief or disbelief in God and religion, the desire are not for children, what each other was looking for in a relationship, descriptions of each other's characters such as open-minded, Reserved, spontaneous, and any other thing that the world considers major building blocks towards relationships and friendships ?

Next, after the relationship was established or made official and remained so for a few months or a year, what was the substance of the communication? Was it not just the usage of words and phrases that you'd heard(love, in love, etc.) but at no time did either you or your love interest define in your conversations what love actually was? Was it not the disclosure of what each other was feeling about certain situations or events in life that affected one in a good or negative way?

Lastly, at some point the relationship marriage or friendship reached a plateau beyond which it could not grow and began to feel stale.

There are a few exceptions of counseling being used as an attempt to fix the problems but it only seemed to work temporarily and then everything returned to the same stale Plateau of no growth.

Sadly ,through all of this there has and will always be some few who keep experiencing the ever-present feeling that there is much more to a connection between two lovers than what one has been experiencing, there is much more to a friendship than what one has been experiencing, or much more to a family than what one has been experiencing.

The question that many have failed to ask is why didn't any of this work even with the communication process being active?

Some think and believe that the communication process wasn't functional because the other in the relationship or friendship wasn't very expressive of their thoughts or feelings beyond insignificant things.

Those kind of thoughts are conceived as if it explains the core reason for the failure of the relationship marriage or friendship as though the fault must be placed solely upon the other with no blame on oneself.

Once again it's stated:

" The Nature in which we approach a thing dictates the nature of the results received"

I know, truth sometimes hurts but when it does, it's always necessary to disengage you from something that you've invested a lot of sentimental and emotional value into that's not only not good to
you but isnt good for you as well.

99.9% of the time the initial spark of interest in another for what one considers a love interest has nothing to do with love. Yes, that physical attraction again.
99.9% of the time we as human beings feel that we are loved only when we are paid attention to, held in someone's arms, giving valuable time, or bought things.

Sadly, this is best termed "The lapdog syndrome " where an individual's idea of love or of being loved is the exact actions that a lapdog craves and receives from its owner. Tender Caresses, treats (gifts), being held, quality time, being provided for (clothing, food, shelter), pedicures, paid hair treatment ,etc.

First of all contrary to what the world has taught you or influenced you to believe, the foundation for any communication process that you could ever attempt to establish between you and others actually begins within you between you and love .Yes that's right ! shocking is it not?

Actually, what people fail to realize even more about love is the fact that love can't exist within you without it suggesting and influencing some thoughts within you
whose very purpose is to be released to others in conversation and communication.

What does that ultimately mean? It ultimately means there is no real or right communication without love being involved when it comes to our search for love in another.

Why? How? Because love as well brings its own language to the table of human experience that utilizes communication as a facilitator of what it has to teach and Implement in a continuous never ending flow
within the minds of the ones under its influence.

A continuous process of communication that ignites thoughts, perceptions, and feelings within one that becomes naturally transmitted to the other, who in return receives those thoughts and allows them to interact with and connect with all that has become embedded within one's memory through experience ,where those deep thoughts originating from love engages and transforms old understandings from old experiences into new, better ,and rightful understandings.
Those rightful understandings about unlimited things are then in return released back (in the form of words) into the thinking of the original one who initiated the expressed thoughts.

Inevitably causing the originator of the expressed thoughts to receive a more elevated version of the thoughts that originated from them but were returned to produce growth.

This is just a general outline of love's communication process that causes a mutual catalyst of continuous growth, rejuvenation, and unification within the minds and hearts of those truly connected by love.

Within this communication process of love, the growth primarily involves the growth of the couple or groups of people connected by love but that unified growth is predicated upon the growth of the individual that it is receives through one's consciousness of love and the redefined experiences it affords the individual so that the benefits of it can be transferred and contributed by each individual into the whole of the connection or relationship with another or others.

When true love is involved between people, the magnitude of love's influence and power within the connection doesn't allow any thoughts or feelings that one is getting tired of the other's presence, the connection is getting old, or that one needs a break from the other.

Why? Or how is that possible? Because love never tires of the object of its focus. Every moment in the presence of the object of its focus is relished as a moment to directly connect with itself within the other person so much so until the other person could just be describing an experience with a fly on the wall and in the ears of the other, it will seem as the greatest expression ever formulated in the world.

Once again, it may be questioned as to why or how that is possible? Simply because of the fact that love redefines and transforms the process of communication into its highest and most significant purpose that produces the highest and most significant and meaningful results.

Love's Redefining and transformation of the communication process establishes communication as the most powerful conduit that facilitates the mutual exchange of pieces of one another's essence with the other or others involved until what is expressed actually becomes a part of the other and begins a continuous mental and soulful process of assimilation within each until each begins to mirror the other at the very core of who they are. Two minds and hearts in sync as one.

The communication process is by no means easy from the very beginning, it as everything else in life must evolve through stages of imperfections, mistakes, and difficulties.

It is love that pulls two or more hearts through those imperfections with love's primary Influenced thought and understanding that each imperfection and mistake made is to be overcome and accepted as necessary steps to equip the one's involved with the greatest tools of life, unbending faith and assurance that as long as the communication is what is, no problem in life will ever be able to approach and survive love's communication process that exists between them.

Infatuation's Delusional Position As Love

The origin of the word infatuation comes from a Latin word (Infatus) which means foolish desire or perception.

Frequently confused with love, infatuation is typified by a strong, fleeting desire that has its roots in idealization and fantasy rather than reality. This deluded mindset causes people to exaggerate and distort the actual existence of the thing or person it is focused upon which undermines relationships.

Infatuation is defined as a foolish desire because the motivating idea behind it is trifling in nature and has no real significance or purpose to it.

The only purpose behind infatuation always amounts to the desire to use ,possess or experience a person, place, or thing for the fulfillment of momentary happiness, sexual pleasure, recreational pursuits, or egotistical endeavors of control over a perceived inferior. Thus many prey upon people of the opposite sex with low self-esteem under the disguise of love.

Disillusionment ,dissatisfaction, and frustration arise when the infatuation fades and the gap widens drastically between the fantasy perception of the person and what the actual reality is concerning this person. When this becomes apparent and undeniable.

Conflicts, misunderstandings, and emotional distress are frequently the outcome of these irrational expectations. Therefore, sincere connection and mutual understanding—two prerequisites for a strong, long-lasting relationship—are compromised by the deluded condition of infatuation.

When you watch soap operas and romance movies or read romance novels and this becomes the blueprint from which you construct your understanding of love, then you are delusional and just infatuated with the idea of love or of being in love and not love itself.

Some are so caught if in their emotions of needing to be noticed by someone or needing to be wanted by someone until they're easily susceptible to the actions of infatuation from another because infatuation can and most times does mimic or project actions associated with caring, being kind, and considerate while in pursuit of its goals.

That is something that may be hard to accept but it needs to be accepted if you truly desire to begin the process of learning to know and understand what love truly is.

We as people need to also learn the difference between liking something and loving something. The two seem so similar to most people until they're used interchangeably to express the idea of just simply enjoying something because of the happy feeling things bring us, but liking and loving present two totally different sets of feelings for two totally different reasons and purposes. One is shallow, the other is at the very essence of things. One is a reaction to something external, the other is the basic foundation of all that is mentally and consciously internal.

CHAPTER 8

Truly Knowing Or Not Knowing, That is the determining Factor

Do you truly know what love is? Is a very hard question for some to answer but then again it's easy for two kinds of people.

1.Those who actually know and understand the reality of love and

**2. Those who foolishly rush to repeat clichés and opther instant microwave statements
they've either read or heard.**

How does one tell the difference? Easily by the actions that reveal the decisions they've made in mind and heart that have no resemblance to right or fairness, some of love's main principles.

The fact of what is truly known or not known is also revealed by the longevity of the things they're parroting but have no experience of.

How so ? because at a short period after the repeating runs out, thus the true substance of (not knowing) will stand revealed where they can't think or relay anything of fact or reality outside of the boundaries of those parroted clichés and statements.

The actions that reveal the fact that one doesn't know is shown in their decisions to continuously look for love according standards and methods that have nothing to do with love or actually producing love.

Revealing actions that demonstrate one considering and choosing others who are no more suitable for love than a bucket of gas is for putting out a raging house fire.

Contrary to the experts and those disguised as knowing love, no amount of loving from one can ever impart a value or need for love into another nor impart a knowledge of love into another.

Why? because love is initially a personal realization that one has to become conscious of themselves through a narrow path of personal experience that teaches and redevelops that one according to the internalized lessons of right attitude, right thinking, right intentions, and right actions becoming solidified into the very heart of who they are until those principles of right are so well grounded in them until the demonstration of them are easily manifested consistently without a minor feeling of a want or need to deter, thereby love is finally awakened.

There are many who will disagree but disagree without one solid base to stand upon. Just a personal feelings and assumptions born out of a want to have love and anything else of true significant value and importance to come easy and in submission to petty human desires to have things instant, without a process, without a requirement of patience & humility, without rules of order that they can't circumvent or manipulate, and the petty human desire & exaggerated egotistical motive to recognize nothing or no one as the ultimate director and controller of that which they want, not even God, The Creator, or Supreme being.

Lastly, the main thing that reveals one as not knowing what love is, is when one is questioned about love and they proceed to define love as existing in one singular (one size fits all things) theoretical way, when in fact, the only way to even begin to answer the question, is actually with another question that in and of itself is the only thing that can give clarity and a point of direction in which to answer appropriately, that question is ....” What degree of love's expressive nature, function, and context are you asking about?

How so? because love isn't just love. There are multiple dimensions of expression (points of meaning, acting & revealing) that love operates from and each has a specific context in which it applies and emanates from.

The context is where many run into problems because they try to apply one context of love to situations that deal with another context like the way people call themselves loving pets or vehicles. It's no joke because the majority of the world's people only feel loved or feel like they're loving others when there exists the acts of taking care of them, spending time with them, feeding them, taking them places, considering their wants, and buying them things to make them look better, or when the acts of caressing and holding are present. The idea of verbal expressions of the love within someone in communication has to take the backseat to the actions even though the consistent and constant verbal expressions of the deeper feelings and perceptions of love that exist in one for them is a rare phenomenon in the world that they've never had or experienced.

There is an even more decisive element that reveals who knows and who doesn't know what love is.

When one truly knows and understands what love is, in a loveless world full of loveless people and loveless situations stemming from those people, those that truly know and understand, either find themselves alone and without a love interest or find themselves moving outward and away from the ones that are only pretending to be capable of loving.

How is that possible? because when love is awakened or already active within self for self, love equips one not only with the necessary inner definition and inner depth of thinking that allows one to approach or be approached, engage, and then analyze any particular person at the very core of who they are with the right questions that are so penetrative until it allows them to be able to rightly determine the extent to which love is either already awakened or still dormant and inactive within a person.

This is how the active presence of love provides one with a precise method of thinking and reacting that helps avoid the unnecessary negative and hurtful situations that another person may pose in regards to a relationship or friendship.

In human relationships, the authentic nature of our interactions can significantly impact the quality and depth of our connections. Yet, people often find themselves pretending to know or understand the central essence of their relationships, often influenced by societal expectations, cultural norms, or personal insecurities.

Pretending in Romantic Relationships

Romantic relationships often originate with a set of assumptions about love, roles, and behaviors, most of which are influenced heavily or predominately by academic assumptions, internet portrayals, television portrayals, cultural traditions, and norms of society.

People may pretend to understand the dynamics of love, thus leading to miscommunication , misunderstandings, and unfulfilled expectations.

1. Assumptions about Love & Its Origins.

Most people in the world base their knowledge and understanding love on observed portrayals in movies, books, and social media. These sources often promote an exaggerated view of love, thus leading individuals to form unrealistic expectations and unrealistic methods to acquire those unrealistic expectations.

2. Consequences Of Pretending in Romantic Relationships

Pretending to understand the dynamics of love can create a superficial connection, where partners are not fully honest about their true intentions and feelings. This most times leads to frustration, resentment, confusion and the inevitable natural demise of a superficial and unrealistic connection.

3. Examples

Consider a couple where one partner believes that extravagant romantic actions are necessary for expressing love, while the other values everyday acts of just spending time together. If both pretend to adhere to the other's expectations without communicating their true stance , the relationship dwindles and ends.

Pretending to Know & Understand Love In Family Structure Dynamics

Family structures are often governed by unspoken rules and expectations based upon assumptions about love and how to apply what is assumed.

Family members may pretend to understand or pretend to be genuinely committed to their roles and responsibilities while situations occur that reveal otherwise ,leading to strained relationships, uncaring words and actions, and sometimes disrespectful words and actions.

1. Family Expectations :The Pressure to Conform to Something One Doesn't Truly Value

In many families, there is an expectation to adhere to certain roles, such as the dutiful parent , the supportive sibling, or the authoritative parent. These roles can be based on cultural norms, family traditions, or personal expectations.

2. Examples of Pretending to know and Understand Love in the Family Structure

For instance, a parent might pretend to be interested in the children's activities to meet their children's expectations but the parent's actions show a bare minimum of interest because of secretly harboring other aspirations. This pretense can lead to frustration and a lack of fulfillment in a family structure.

Example:

3.Impact On Family Bonds and Communication

When family members pretend to know and understand what love is, it can lead to misunderstandings and a lack of true connection.

This can exaggerate family bonds and create a sense of fakeness that forces the genuine at heart family members to separate themselves from those family members who generate the fakeness or this can foster a family environment where no word is perceived as dependable and nobody is perceived as dependable or caring in the situations where a family member needs another family member the most.

That is another element within the origins of gangs in society that society refuses to acknowledge as their fault.

Most dysfunctional families are dysfunctional for various reasons that originate from simple misplaced attitudes :

1. Grown ups who think and feel that a parents love doesn't mean having to listen to the children or that the children are their robots or some human A.I android figure to be programmed and regarded as possessing no thoughts or feelings that matter.
2. Children (especially teenagers) who always think they're grown before their time and are always in disagreement and at odds with rules of the house and punishment.

The parents or guardians of such children are most times only at fault when they misperceive their love as requiring them to force children into submission by any means.

This type of response is a result of a misplaced attitude that they know what's best for them better than they do which is always true but necessitating a different method.

Love in this family context isn't always about enforcement , its more so about loving this type of child or children enough to realize and remember what it was like to be that age and just because the grownup's parent or parents methods worked with them , it doesn't mean that method is appropriate for a new generational child or children.

Sometimes even though the grown up feels they love this type of conflicting child or children , love in its most simplistic and realest terms dictates that you have to allow the child or children to experience the harsh and cruel consequences of their own disobedience that the world will inevitably bring upon them.

That's not saying to abandon them or restrict them from your care and concern but in dire situations as that, the best way to implement that care and concern is with unconditional positive advice and encouragement.

A major lesson has to be learned that the grown up can't learn for the disobedient children.

That lesson is, The main and most significant difference between grown ups and children is experience and the knowledge and understanding of things that can only come by experience.

1. What basically will work and what won't work
2. What thoughts and actions are more prone to lead to positive results and which one's more prone to lead to trouble, harm, or dissatisfaction

3. The full and complete extent of the dangers and dangerous people that await outside of the child's or children's bedroom, school environment, and neighborhood.

4. The main reason why some children excel in life more easily and less complicated than others even though they have the same or similar intelligence.

   That determining factor being that the easily excelled listen to and incorporate the benefits of their parent's guidance and its knowledge, understanding, and experience into their thoughts and decisions so that they're prepared to confidently and efficiently approach and overcome life's difficulties and problems with ease based upon what their parent or parents taught them and their trust in their parents guidance as the best course of thought and action in order to achieve success more so than their own limited, inexperienced, and incomplete ideas and perceptions about life.

To watch a child of yours make mistakes that are thoughtless and sometimes dangerous will never be easy or comfortable and do so is never unloving or heartless, it's a decision born out wisdom that knows that no amount of talk, fussing, or punishment will detour a conflicting and disobedient child from running their head into a wall that they're determined to challenge with a stubborn head.

A lot of parents and family members just give up on other family members who at some point are rebellious, criminal minded, promiscuous, or stubborn and many there are who have changed for the better and became successful from even the most lowest of positions in life like jail or prison.

That is a lesson in itself, Love never prejudges anyone because all have the potential to change in time and the length of how long it takes isn't up to another, the only choice that reak love naturally influences them make is to be an unconditionally loving support with an undying faith in that family member's ability to change.

Not many family are capable of learning that lesson because they didn't possess any real love to give in the first place.

Such unloving family relations should never be a hindrance or discouragement , it should be rather a motivation to stand on one's on two feet ,to succeed in spite of the unloving family relation , and to become greater by being all that they were not to another who was or is in that same position or another who just simply needs someone to be there as that dependable element they've never had but always desperately needed.

Pretending To Know & Understand Love In Friendships

Friendships are often said by the experts to be built on shared interests and mutual ideals without a single mention of love.

However, it is the superficial expectations of love and assumptions about love that lead to false pretenses eroding the condition of these

friendships that were doomed to fail from their very beginning because they lacked any real substance of love but were rather based upon temporary principles of thought and action.

Society often influences the idea or standard of how friendships should

 look and operate while society (government, religious congregations ,social groups etc.)

itself shows in everyday dealings that they only consider friendships to be situations of benefit or compliance which leads the normal average individuals to assume they know what a friendship is composed of based upon that standard of the world.

This usually includes being constantly available, open to persuasion and manipulation, or engaging in certain activities under false pretenses.

These type of friendships are always superficial and based upon things of no real significance or importance such as a mutual enjoyment for gossip, drinking or using intoxicants, going to clubs, etc.

The Effects Of Pretending That One Knows & Understands Love In Friendships

When friends pretend to know and understand things that are important to others , it can erode trust.

Being authentic is crucial for building loyalty, a deep, meaningful, and lasting connection that only love can provide.

Psychological & Emotional Effects Of Pretending To Know & Understand Things We don't

Pretending to understand or know certain things that one does not can and will create stress upon an individual's mental health and emotional well-being.

The constant effort to maintain a lie can lead to stress, anxiety, and a feeling of inadequacy. An individual may struggle with their self-worth and experience a wide range of emotional fatigue.

The Emotional Ramifications Of Pretending To Know & Understand Something

Pretending to know and understand something can create an emotional burden. Individuals may feel isolated, vulnerable, misunderstood, and unable to be their true selves.

The Role Of Society Norms In Facilitating False Assumptions

1. Social norms often attempt to dictate how people think, feel, and act as well as define how relations should be, thus leading or pressuring individuals to conform to these standards even if they do not coincide with their true selves.

This perpetuates a cycle of false pretenses and blocks any possibility of any genuine human relations.

The assuming and false pretense dilemma about love as well rests at the heart of the dysfunction called racism.

There is a very significant perception that most people in the world have about love that stems from ignorance and selfishness.

The belief that we as individuals can define and direct our love in any way that best suits us as individuals and places everything beyond our individuality as a nonessential to love.

One of the most significant things that a lot of people have failed to pay attention to is the fact that even when you look at all of the major religions of the world and even the smaller offshoot branches of religion, none of their religious scriptures ever actually define love in any definitive terms or details, its either in superficial ways that describe what love produces or just the mention of love but never the exact definition of what love is in and of itself.

There is one particular verse " God is Love" that many focus upon as if thinking " oh yeah, that's the definition of love" while truly missing the universality of the statement that applies to all things.

Unknowingly, according to the specific principle contexts of all things' creation and the nature of their design, there are and always will be natural dictates that certain prerequisites be present before one can even approach and begin to possess a minute understanding of love, God, and the specific predetermined aims , directions , purposes and functions therein that each naturally influences within things when the things are existing in their natural context rather than the contexts shaped, fashioned, and directed by modern man.

This may be becoming a little complicated to some, more complicated than what some have imagined or expected but in reality that complicated feeling or perception isn't really about the content that is being expressed or about to be expressed, the feeling or perception that something is being made complicated actually derives from a simplistic mindstate that most of the world have been influenced to have and act from thereby creating a mental, emotional, spiritual and behavioral box of confinement.

A confinement that keeps one in a perpetual self-inflicted shallow consciousness that not only believes that all things are simple without a deeper meaning, significance, or understanding but as well a consciousness that only seeks that which seems simplistic.

Why? in order to avoid having to do the one thing that actually determines positions and conditions of living. Simply thinking, analyzing, and measuring things for one's self beyond the immediate appearance.

Sadly, it is the surface thinkers where most assumptions are easily accepted and transmitted into their dealings with others, thus the exact reason why dysfunctions are so widely spread in the world. Most of the time people don't even think about the fact of whether or not there could be some serious consequences attached to the decisions we make.

We as people naturally think it's okay to approach and deal with things with very little or no knowledge and understanding at all about what we're preparing to engage.

Why? Because of the belief that as long as we're sincere, everything will turn out fine. In truth there's nothing as worse and dangerous than sincere ignorance because even though damage or hurt may be produced within what we're dealing with, there's an underlying idea that things can be fixed or changed in time if we only have faith or as long as we continue doing our best.

CHAPTER 5

The Contexts Of Love : The Foundation Of ALL Human Relations

This next chapter will deal with those different contexts that factually go against the grain of everything that has been ever taught and influenced by modern man in the last 3000 plus years.

Whether you believe in a God, Supreme Being, Creator etc. or not. Each particular creation has its own particular nature as when it comes to that which we know as male and female.

According to the principles of the perception about individualized love, the particular individuals always perceive love as originating from one's own individual self and basically applying predominantly and exclusively to one's own individual self. The defining point in that matter is, if you do not know and understand the exact totality of what individual self is composed of and you only have a fraction of it ,then you're only going to be able to understand and demonstrate who you are in a limited partial capacity.

The direct consequential effect of a partial function is the drastic altering and rearranging of a natural process such as Male-female

relationships and family structures into that which is unnatural, defective, and counterproductive.

When it comes to a context being applied to anything or something existing within a context, it simply means the analysis of a thing with numerous surrounding factors involved like environment, habits, and natural inclinations to arrive at a more precise and more complete understanding of a thing.

Simple analogies are :

1. **If someone wanted to know or understand something about a specific high speed automobile then, the request would be for information on an automobile within the context of a Ferrari.**

2. If someone wanted to truly know, understand, and experience the true nature and natural function of a lion, they wouldn't go to a zoo, why because a lion in a zoo is positioned in an unnatural environment of a caged confinement which is a context.

To see a lion's natural function and nature in action, it would have to be in the context of its natural unconfined habitat or environment in Africa.

Within the context of Male/Female relationships, each gender is analyzed according to the ancient origins of each and the original positions , functions, and natures that was originally applied to each as well as demonstrated by each.

This is an area that has historically been intentionally mislabeled as myths by a world that wanted to supplant these histories with its own distorted and deceptive stories and histories about the origin of things.

Why ? so that a new paradigm of new definitions and standards could be implemented to reposition everything and everyone in the world into submission to the designs of Eurocentric minds and Eurocentric influences that would perpetually remake the world's people (especially people of dark skin or dark skin origins) in the image of the Europeans and the designated thinking and position of inferiority based upon a manufactured disconnect from who they truly were.

It has always been the most logic and truth defying event of how people of dark skin or dark skin origins could be influenced to view their own histories about the origins of things as myths and something to be disliked or ignored but at the same time be influenced even in modern times to wholeheartedly accept someone else's histories about the origins of things

So-called histories like Adam and Eve that was borrowed from their very own histories and has all the elements that are said to define something as a myth but can't and won't consider it as a baseless myth even though it exists with no historical or archeological ties to any ancient times it claims to describe.

Is that false or a lie? Is that the sign of a uncover Bible hater ?

No, it's the sign and most powerful indication of an extreme history lover and researcher who studies ALL histories from ALL races of people without one natural bias or prejudgment.

The fact remains that the book of Genesis or Bara' sit in Hebrew, has records about itself and the time in which it was first documented, catalogued, and made to be scripture and its not only not ancient at all but also there's no original ancient manuscript scrolls or pieces of a ancient scroll for it from the time period that Genesis describes. There is only pieces of scrolls specifically dated from the time in which Yeshua (Jesus) supposedly lived.

The Dead Sea Scrolls aren't even ancient scrolls. They're also from the time period in which Yeshua (Jesus) supposedly lived.

Why is this significant? To defend the only real histories that are ancient enough to give someone the original natures, functions , and relationships of Male and female so that the original dynamics can realized and used as measuring principle to understand the root origins and causes of the dysfunctions.

Context significantly impacts our understanding of gender,.

It is the lack of such that has ensured a continuance and reinforcing of intentional misleading misinterpretations.

It is the current cultural, social, and educational factors who derive their base and standards of measurement and definition from Eurocentric influences that continue to transmit misperceptions and deceit about Male/ Female natures, roles and their proper relationships.

Without considering these contexts, one might misunderstand the nature, function, and purpose of gender, reinforcing stereotypes and biases that distort the complexities of male-female interaction.

Those particular relations were meant to incorporate each of the female and male essences within their natural respective positions and roles of thought, feeling, and identity as equal contributors to the relations in which humans would interact but according to the nature of each.

When it comes to the very basis of life itself , human life, or even other things in the universe. There is always a natural context attached to it that facilitates the way such things will behave and function in continuous cycles, a natural environment it will exist within, specific acts it will perform , and certain actions it produces to naturally align it with other things it is meant to be connected to in order to produce other elements within a system of nature or the universe. The human being is no different or exempt from such principles of existence.

Most people have a limited knowledge therefore limited understanding of the historical precedents of love and how it was originally defined, demonstrated, facilitated and maintained.

Unknowingly to the mass majority of the world, when it came to ancient civilizations and the particular knowledge that they possessed in reference to the human being.

Within the very languages that connected them, there was always a feminine and masculine element attached to the very words and physical objects that they utilized and interacted with. Such words as earth, wind , spirit, energy, sound, and even the life force and the mind itself are all feminine since it was considered spirit and energy.

(Source: Ancient Hebrew language Encyclopedia)
Not affiliated with altered texts or words as promoted by every one of the UnSemitic Jewish Society Publications. Who applies unancient European definitions of the Yiddish language & other European cultures to modern unancient Hebrew words.

How are these things relevant to love? Because it gives one a more precise knowledge and understanding of not only what love is but also gives one the precise knowledge and understanding of how love was facilitated and the understanding of the differences in human relations when these contexts are acknowledged and implemented.

It is a well-worn out cliché that says "one must love self first before being able to love others". But if you do not know or understand what the individual self actually is composed of, then it can be said that you do not even know how to begin to love oneself.

Any person's given name is not that particular person's actual identity.

Each human it's going to be either female or male first.

Each female or male is not the original first female or male so this dictates that no modern Male or female can define themselves and their very nature according to their own definitions and be right.

If one looks and studies into the ancient civilizations like the Sumerian, Egyptian ,and the Indus Valley Civilizations, one would readily see an acute difference in the cultural norms from those of modern times.

Cultural differences involving what is termed male and female and these particular differences were the defining points that actually allowed these civilizations to have

better quality and better positioned relations without all of the dysfunctions that are now experienced in the modern world for the last past three to four thousand years.

Ultimately the questions are what did these particular civilizations and people know and understand that modern people don't know and understand? How does that show and prove a significant difference?

What those particular civilizations in history show even in the before mentioned languages and perceptions is a true, positive, effective, and efficient relation between the so-called female and male.

Within these civilizations is the exact nature of the particular male and female and how these particular elements were not just existing as what we know as male and female but were distributed all throughout nature on various levels that were highly significant in the overall functioning of all living and material things.

When it comes to those particular elements or essences that are considered male and female, these are modern terms that has been placed upon these particular essences by men in history with the ulterior motive of hiding and also redefining the knowledge of the female's true identity so that an exclusive male dominance paradigm could come into existence.

A new Masculine paradigm where the being mislabeled as female ,would become repositioned from a state of equality into a position of inferiority and under control, thus the creation of an imbalance and dysfunction within the Male-female relationships and the family structure.

How so? Because in all of the major ancient languages that which is known as female was considered to be an feminine energy and power that was different but never inferior to that which is considered to be the masculine energy or male existence.

If you look at words in the Hebrew language such as the act and power of creation, it is a feminine energy and power. Also if you look at the word "love" in Hebrew and Sumerian and other ancient languages the word love is always feminine. This is the reason why in many of the ancient languages and cultures, like Egyptian, Summer, Indus valley, or even the latter civilizations as Greek, Hebrew, and Roman, love is personified in the form of a female figure.

Hathor - Egyptian

Ishta - Sumerian

Radha - India (Indus Valley)

Xochiquetzal - Aztec

Ma-Tsu - Asia (modern China)

Benten - Asia (modern Japan)

Ixchel - Mayan

Inanna - Sumerian

Astarte - Sumerian

Freya - Norseman (the origin of the week day Friday)

Aine - Celtic

Asherah - Original Hebrew

Many people have been given a misconception and misinterpretation of these ancient histories and teachings in order to facilitate a lie that these cultures worshiped statues in order to deter minds from looking back there and finding the truth.

Why was this personification of love in the form of a female very significant even now? Because it gives one a knowledge, understanding and perception of love in its most powerful forms that determines a lot in the realm of humans.

How so? Because the first love that any human being ever comes into contact with is from that of his or her mother while in the womb of this mother.

Not only was the love of a woman in ancient times considered to be second to only that of the Creator but it was also considered to be the most powerful and the only unconditional love in the human realm that did not have to go through a particular process in order to exist ,it was natural for a mother to love the child just simply because it was a part of her and began to exist within her.

So there is evidence that love is not just simply love and that it does have a context through which it operates ,functions , and is to be facilitated and that is according to the nature of the individual in which love has become awakened.

Therefore, the love that is facilitated through that which is known as a feminine essence is expressed and implemented within all human relations according to that which the feminine nature has to specifically impart and so forth also with the male or masculine essence.

When it comes to that which we know as female and woman, these are titles that originated from a Eurocentric culture and psychological mind frame that was bent on redefining the gender known as woman to a position of inferiority within a new paradigm of Male dominance that was of Eurocentric origins.

From Roman General/ Conqueror Scipio Africanus, King Minos of Crete , Roman General/ Emperor Julius Caesar, Roman General/ Emperor Hadrian, Alexander The Great, Emperor Constantine, and The Maykop Caucasian Civilization (The oldest of Caucasian Civilizations).

All of these Caucasian Conquerors and Civilizations had two things in common

1) A hatred for women and social/Political norms to deprive women of any rights, designate women as property belonging to their husbands, a theology that women were on the intellectual level with children and much more.

2) A well defined political norm that defined all non members of those Caucasian Civilizations as worthy to be nothing but slaves & Never Citizens.

- A dislike for Dark skinned people. (References: Online Britannica Encyclopedia, Heilbrunn Timeline of Art History (The Met) online,

How can that be? It is so because the majority of the world's cultures and civilizations in Asia and so-called Africa weren't Patriarchal in nature, they were Bi - archal which means shared or naturally co-ruled by both genders.

So what is the point of all of this? The main point is that the titles such as female and woman were designed to not only Implement a state of mind but also a teaching and condition that would exemplify the idea that that which is known as the feminine person (female) would be defined only by that which is determined by male or man , this in itself inferred that the woman didn't have any separate existence or foundation in nature that was not defined or determined by man.

Fe - male = feminine version of man

Wo - man = vagina version of man (as "wo" signifies womb (a vagina)

One might ask why aren't those particular titles correct or proper, when they are supported by the biblical story of Adam and Eve?

The answer to that is quite simple. When dealing with stories or information and other languages words and situations can be lost in the translation when trying to translate words and cultures into different languages other than the ones they were meant for.

As a matter of fact the story of Adam and Eve in the Bible are actually names and a story that was borrowed from a much older source and civilization (India).

Found in :

1. (The Prophecies) Translated by: Ramutsariar.

2. Adam & Eve's Sumerian Origins
    (Epic of Gilgamesh
" Sacred plant in garden that grants eternal youth and guarded by serpent."

    " Enki (God of wisdom) creates a garden and a human in it named Adamu that he creates from dust of the earth "

3. The Tahitan Creation Story " Their God Taaroa put men to sleep ,during which he pulled a bone Ivi (Eve) from one of them and it became a woman.

Whose version happens to be over six thousand years older than the particular version that is explained in English in the Bible where the original version has the names as Adama and Heva in a garden with a tree of life and a serpent of a different nature than the one in the old Testament scriptures.

Even Within the scriptures of the Hebrew in the Old Testament, what is translated in the English is not even close to what is said in the Hebrew when it comes to the origins of Adam and Eve.

Unknowing to many the name "Adam" itself derives from a Hebrew word " Adama " which is feminine. "Adama" means "earth" but when it comes to the story of Adam and Eve it does not represent literal objects like soil or situations, the story of Adam and Eve is symbolical of principles of power, principle natures of things, principal positions in relation to The Creator and principles of conduct so earth or soil is a principle.

"Adama" is a principal energy of the creation process which signifies that it was an essential foundational element of the physical and inner existence of the form that became known as human (Adam).

Ultimately meaning that that which became the physical manifestation of Eve , actually existed before Adam as an intricate element of the Creator that proves a feminine element is as much an equal part of the Creator as the masculine element is.

This is proven by the very first name of God that appears in Genesis (Elohim). "Elohim" is plural and was originally translated with the nature of that pluralism being defined as feminine and Masculine.

This is a fact that has disturbed the new converters to Judaism for the past 2,000 + years until they redacted much of the Hebrew scriptures to translate and eliminate the original anthropomorphism from it and the feminine characteristics of God from it.

This is seen in the modern Jewish Rabbinical writings and the extent they've been willing to go to misdirect away from the truth.

That extent is a bold willingness to lie and say those very scriptures show Yahweh as the first God mentioned and that Eloha or Elohim was a later addition from Canaanite influences.

As usual with liars and deceivers who always wish and intend to rewrite history in their favor or rewrite history to include them where they otherwise were never mention or existed.

There isn't and never was an ancient people named Canaanites.

As a matter of fact, there's no ancient recordings or archeological evidence of there ever being a Canaanite race of people or a Canaanite political, religious, or social group calling themselves Canaanites or being called that by anyone in any of the histories of the ancient nations that occupied the so-called Mesopotamia or middle East.

A Civilization was discovered in the middle East in 1928 and was named (Ugarit) but sometimes called (Ras Shamra) and the first thing the converted Judaic Nation of Israel and its Rabbis and Christian flunkies did was start proclaiming that The Ugarit Civilization and the Ugarit Texts that were found was the long lost Canaanites.

Factually, NOTHING that was found in what became named Ugarit ever mentioned a Canaanite people or called themselves such. As liars and deceivers normally do, they just threw a name at it and said **" Oh, we found it validating that name and the existence of the Canaanite People we've been looking for."**

(Reference Book: **The triumph of Elohim, From Yahwehisms To Judaisms, By : Diana V. Edelman).**

This reference book contains numerous top Biblical Historians and scholars who present indisputable evidential facts both archeological and ancient texts that contradict everything about the modern mainstream propaganda about what the Hebrew Religion historically consisted of.

It also proves that "Asherah" was more prevalent as a belief than the temple version of Judaism which was for the educated, not the average Hebrews.

Thus also in those same biblical scriptures it is said that they both (male & female) were called "Adam."

The ultimate question is where is this particular expression found to be a fact in nature and the natural functioning of a living organism? and what would change if such was proven to be a fact?

That answer is also very simple. In ancient times there was a specific mind shattering reason as to why the act or process of creation was of a feminine essence and that particular feminine expression of love was considered to be second to only that of the creator but yet divine in nature.

The reason is, because if you look at the very process that enables the continuation of the human species ,you will see at the very heart of it a particular element of creation in childbirth that mimics the power of the Creator to create.

A process of originating within her a unique human. A divine process that actually determines the very nature and foundation of all human thought processes and all foundations of thought to be found in the human being ,right there within her who is called the female.

What you see in childbirth on the outside is nothing compared to what is actually taking place on the inside of the female. What you don't see is that the development of the child is directly connected to the thinking of the female, so much so until the very thoughts of the mother are what influences the brain cells in the unborn child.

What does this ultimately mean? It means exactly what the ancient teachings of the ancient civilizations knew, which is that cultures and civilizations are not defined by the man but by the woman because it is the woman through which all humans must come and must be initially influenced by.

As the woman is the first teacher of all humans and the determiner of the potentials that each and every child will possess or not possess based upon the nature of her thinking while the child is being developed during pregnancy.

The ancient people and their ancient civilizations all knew one fact that would destroy the egotistical and exaggerated false psychological mind frame of modern man.

That explosive fact was and still is :

" The world of people pray for change and Saviors and the answers to those particular prayers have always come through the woman who gives birth to that special person destined to produce that change in the affairs of men and that person isn't and NEVER will be always be a man."

When it comes to the way in which love manifests itself, there are not only contexts through which it expresses itself and makes itself known, there is as well stages of development within these contexts that are to be followed and implemented within a process of growth that one can not and will not escape.

1. **Only the knowledge of Self can lead and qualify one to love self & then others.**
2. **Truly loving others naturally establishes loving relationships with others.**

3. **Loving others is influenced by love to produce relationships that produce family of the same race and friends.**
4. **Families through love naturally connect and combine to construct communities of the same race.**
5. **Communities of a race are Influenced by love to connect at the very essence and to think, act, decide, and judge in accordance with the collective consciousness that is produced for the self - preservation, self-determination, and self- advancement of the race.**

These are the natural basic structural contexts of love that love naturally influences, everything else is built upon and around these.

Everything except the contexts of Gender and race, truth and right, respect and empathy, and justice and accountability, duty and responsibility, and loyalty and commitment which are defining context cornerstones in the structural context.

CHAPTER 6

Love's Test Of Qualification :Through The Fire & Flames Of Experience

Most people are fascinated with the idea of love, being in love ,and even being loved but very few are actually able to commit themselves to the struggles and Imperfections that must be endured in order to reach what is termed love.

Once again , the event of the microwave age in which we live is brought to your mind because when it comes to love as stated multiple times before ,the average person today thinks that love is something instant as if they can wake up one morning and say **"oh I am in love, i know what love is ,or I Feel Love."**

For someone to come along and express the idea that people cannot have love the instant they decide to possess love like some Hocus Pocus magic is involved.

That very thing is sure to cause some severe agitation and aggravation within a lot of people to the point where they want to scream :

" Why can't i have love like that ? or why can't love work that way ,if I
want it to ?"

The answer is quite simple and in accordance with human nature which dictates that :

"No human being can or will truly know or understand a particular thing themselves without experience being involved "

"Someone can tell you anything and it may be the truth to them but until you actually experience it for yourself ,what you were told, is only a statement with the possibility of being true."

Automatically, what comes to mind next is another question which is why would one need to have some type of experience before being able to know or understand love?

This may be a little hard to accept or understand but once again in accordance with human nature "No human being can fully appreciate something without having first experienced certain conditions and circumstances over and over again through a protracted period of time with the exact opposite of what is desired."

In this case, the exact opposite of what love is.
Why is that so ? Because only by experiencing the exact opposite of love can one not only grow into a unconditional appreciation for love but also grow into an unconventional application of love which is where things like preferences, the need to control, and conditional intent dies.

In the realm of human behavior and activities, nothing solidifies a thing within us as an unchangeable principle more so than the tragic and excruciating experiences that we find ourselves creating for ourselves by having the wrong ideas and making the wrong decisions that naturally result from those wrong ideas.

With experience this is not always the case because experience acts as a two tipped flame that can burn you so that all of the unnatural impurities can be released and eliminated or experience can burn you and leave an internal wound to the heart so deep and vast until the hurtful effects of the experience become infected and worsened.

How so ? Infected and worsened by way of particular emotional reactions that are produced such as resentment, hate, and the need to primarily blame the other person for the experience.

That is the most common reaction, rather than looking at the experience for what it is, a lesson taught and a lesson learned that has only resulted in a deeper outcome that was to make one a better, deeper, and wiser, person because it and it's gift has cemented within one the inability to ever have the same ideas and make the same mistakes again.

Experience also has a way of internally changing a person from a previous position of character ,mind State, and behavior that naturally repositions them to be a totally different person and thereby a perfect match for someone whom love has truly awakened whom they weren't previously compatible with in their previous state.

Compatible at the essence where it truly matters.

Experience and the intricate workings of love within has a way of having to allow us to go through some painful experiences over and over again until we are forced to let go of things that we have become sentimentally attached to that unknowingly to us are a hindrance to our development in the right direction.

What right direction? That very positive right direction that more times than anything else isn't about what where we want to grow but about how and where we need to grow in order to qualify for the balance in life that only love can initiate, nurture, and produce.

What balance in life? That balance of thinking and doing that which is not only good to us but good for us. That balance of finally acquiring that which is not only good to us but good for us as well.

It is experience and the many mistakes we make in life that are there to teach us and guide us into improving in the areas in which mistakes were made.

This is a hard lesson for most people to become aware of or to even begin to learn and by their own stubborn persistence in ego tripping, selfishness, and ignorance, end up missing the very things they claim to want or need.

Those most meaningful things such as a true experience with true love. An experience that very few actually realize starts within themselves through a correction of themselves that only experiences can influence.

Love doesn't come easy because there is always a price that one has to pay in order to truly have love awakened in us so that we can see through the eyes of love rather than through the lenses of our own short sightedness and imperfections.

That cost is the sacrifice of every single element of an emotional and psychological immaturity gained from our prior tunnel visioned perceptions and conclusions about the nature of our past experiences.

There's a point while in the midst of our seemingly heartbreaking and soul ripping experiences where we have numerous moments of thinking about giving up on the idea of love or being truly loved.

It is from somewhere deep inside of us there always seems to be a small urging that keeps pushing us to try again.

Sometimes we go through a period of trying to ignore it or bury it by focusing on work or things to occupy our mind and time but time and again that small urging keep pushing us to not give up on love.

Unknowingly to us, that is the small spark of love within us pushing us to continue the experience so that it can finally be realized and fully awakened in us through the conscious mind learning the hardest but most significant lessons in life that rests as the sole key to love's awakening.

"Regardless of what the external world and its unloving people do to me, I love myself enough to never again give the world the power to determine my worth, my potential, or whether i will or won't be loved. "

" The love in me lets me know that it is enough until its other half is through being developed and positioned by time and experience especially for me."

"The power of love in me for me and the power of faith and patience it gives me is stronger than the power of any hurt, disappointment, disrespect, or misuse the world could ever cause me."

While in the midst of our numerous experiences in the course of our lifetime, it becomes easy sometimes to focus more on the pain and the seemingly damage that it does to us more so than the positive things that are always there accompanying the negative things in the different human relations.

So much so until sometimes it's easy to believe that we're destined to be hurt and disappointed over and over again without an end in sight.

Surprisingly, what we fail to realize is that even though each time that we are hurt by someone it seems to go deeper and deeper for a reason.

While in the mist of excruciating pain disappointment and confusion of being hurt, it is not easy at all to realize that the negative has a counterpart that is actually equally positive and outweighs any significance that the negative could ever pose towards us.

How? Because with every experience that involves our hearts, the intensity of what is felt grows stronger and stronger and within every one of those experiences we are exposed to different higher degrees of certain elements both positive and negative that gives us glimpses of the one that life, experience, and love is preparing for us.

The positive being the higher degree of the right and healthy things that will be experienced and the negative being a higher tool of influence that helps shape, mold, and fashion the highest standard of positive measurement within us toward others. " Treat others as we want to be treated".

The negative side of any relationship or any other human relation gives one the ultimate reason for not doing such to others, because we know and understand how it feels and therefore can't and won't do it to others.

Sadly, it seems that there is a reverse effect with many of the world where the negativity incurred within relationships or other human relations influences quite a number of people to turn up the heat and Flames in their experiences by choosing to allow the negativity within their experiences to influence them to feel that they must inflict as much pain ,disappointment, and suffering upon others as it has been inflicted upon them which only increases the power and intensity of the negative situations that such ones will attract for themselves.

This is a very pivotal point in any of our lives where numerous lessons are materializing in our lives through experiences that naturally include other people or things we do in of ourselves that hurt us , disappoint, and frustrate us with the effect of always confusing us or either angering us.

During the trials, tests, and sometimes crushing predicaments that life's experiences takes us through, we never realize and do the one main thing that all contrary and contradicting experiences are trying to force us to do for our own good and benefit,

Simply just stop, take time, and reflect upon the one main element that has the power to change the nature of the experience and eliminate it altogether, the changing of our minds ,the nature of our approach to life and the changing of our perceptions of things, situations, places, people and our methods involved towards all of those things.

Why? Because to change your thoughts and mind is to redefine who you are and the nature of your position & power.

CHAPTER 7

The Fruits Of Experience & True Emotional Empowerment

(Emotional Clarity)

Experience is a multifaceted thing that serves as a teacher through our life experiences, revealing invaluable lessons to us about the consequences of our wrongful decisions. At the very center of our experiences, is the workings to expose our vulnerabilities and insecurities, producing a space where we are more likely to encounter people, things, and situations that challenge our judgment.

These experiences, although often painful and very disappointing, are essential to reshaping our thoughts, beliefs, and understanding into a necessary growth.

When we make decisions in the context of feeling, we are driven by emotions that are prone to cloud our rational thinking. This leads to crucial mistakes, such as trusting the wrong kind of people, making sacrifices that are not reciprocated, or staying in unhealthy relationships out of fear or misplaced attachment.

At no time during any situation are you powerless to change or modify the conditions and events in which you participate or live.

Within the diameter of all relationships, friendships and other relations such as family. It takes the difficulties and problems within these particular relations to actually help us to understand not only our connection to others but the connection that others have with us and what that connection means to them from their individual perspective.

Most times it takes connected people having to go through difficulties and problems along with the sometimes heart wrenching emotional stages of fragility and inner turmoil in order for us to gain a better and deeper grasp of who we are as individuals and our prescribed contribution to the ones we are connected to.

Sometimes it is the excruciating experience within our connections with others that influences us to think that we must isolate ourselves from the one or ones whom we are connected with and in doing so there is always the high probability that our isolation from the particular ones that we are connected with, will deepen the gap between us if love isn't allowed to do what it does best.

Love influences and establishes boundaries in our hearts and minds that always inevitably restricts our thoughts and actions from causing hurt and damage to the ones we are connected to so that any feeling of a need to isolate ourselves from the ones we love is only brief and never prolonged.

It takes these difficulties to arrive at a better understanding of our connections with others and our primary duty and obligation of love to the others to contribute love in its purest form to aid, assist, and support them in maintaining the connection or re-establishing their position within the connection even their failings, doubts, or confusion may involve our very own selves.

It takes the heat and pain of misunderstandings and miscommunications to teach us the true value of the others involved and ourselves.

There's nothing like the power of love and the faith it inspires to stand strong and relentless in our pursuits to allow our love to encourage and heal others whom we are connected to even when the world has given up on them.

Through the fire of experience verily one finds the true power of Love that is relentless and all persevering in regards to the one our love is focused on and connected to.

The teachings of love that are offered through experience give us a deeper insight into the intricate workings of Love within our hearts and Minds that otherwise would not be discovered and incorporated into who we are for the expressed benefit of helping and supporting others to empower themselves.

We learn through the severe tests and trials of experience that we can never force by might or petty bickerings a necessary change that our loved ones may desperately need because we can never make the changes for them, love's role and purpose is to exist as the ultimate unconditional encourager and supporter until love and its realization awakens in others that we are connected to.

Sometimes the fire of experiences forces us to realize that the one or ones we are connected to need other things other than us to become better and the connection isn't for us.

Surprisingly, of the rarest nature, love sometimes through another accomplishes that miraculous event of encouraging and influencing the needed betterment in the one or ones that are loved.

It is the nature of love and its position in our overall connection to others that determines whether the connection is right or wrong for us.

We as humans according to our proclivity to make mistakes as an element of learning and understanding, can never force our feelings to be love when they are not nor force our mere feelings into the power of love when such feelings don't and can't even come close to doing so.

That delusional frame of perception and feeling is and shall always be a highly favored means by the uninformed that only makes things worse for themselves and others.

If nothing else, experience will inevitably force one to know whether they truly know what love is by the measure of them either continuing in the dysfunctions or the measure of them resolving the dysfunctionalities of their lives and relations with others by them finally having love awakened within them.

No matter what our opinions are, experience has a way of showing us our the errors of our misguided thoughts and feelings, it is very few who actually pay attention, most have to create and go through an emotionally and mentally torturous cycle of their own making before they learn.

Contrary to our usual perceptions while in the midst of wrongful and hurtful experiences, the wrongful decisions we made to arrive at that point are not just errors; they represent opportunities for us where we are compelled to initiate some pivotal introspection of ourselves.

The pain and regret that always seem to follow our mistakes forces us to reflect on our actions and their impacts on ourselves and others.

Through this reflection, we find better understanding and insights into our priorities, boundaries, and needs.

Experience, therefore, aims to teach us resilience and the importance of self-respect and self-awareness. Each experience of heartbreak or disappointment is a lesson in determining what is truly important and not important in relationships , what basic decisions naturally lead to the mistakes, and how to better direct our emotions and choices in the future.

Furthermore, in this way, experience not only highlights our wrongful decisions but also guides us towards growth, helping us to make wiser and more informed choices in our relationships.

Through experience, it is meant for us to learn the greater lessons of integrity, self-worth, the enduring strength of faith and the true value and importance of what it means to be well informed.

EMOTIONAL RESPONSIBILITY

Experience serves as the most powerful instructor in emotional responsibility whereas it guides us into making choices that are more in alignment with truth and right when we engage in relationships.

Experience exposes us to a wide range of emotions and scenarios that challenge our current faulty and counterproductive decision-making process and influences us to replace them with those decision-making skills that limit or eliminate the power and influences of negative people in our lives and the negative situations that come with them.

Our experiences, both painful and enjoyable, are very instrumental in teaching us the consequences of our actions and the importance of making choices that uphold principles more suitable towards producing positive outcomes for ourselves and those whom we encounter.

At the heart of those experiences is the intent to equip us with a new standard of judgment that truly allows one to see themselves for the very first time and the total cause and effect of wrongful decisions—whether it be through dishonesty, neglect, or selfishness—we not only harm others but also ourselves.

Such choices tend to create emotional turmoil and guilt, revealing the negative impact of our actions on our well-being and the integrity of who we are.

These painful outcomes serve as crucial lessons that highlight the importance of emotional responsibility.

CHAPTER 8

The Nature & Influence Of Love

This is the moment that's been highly anticipated. So without hesitation, lets enter this slowly.

Disclaimer :

At No time during what is expressed beyond this point should the reader take what is given as though it is bringing him or her into the actual state or condition of knowing this as the truth.

Why? Because it is the truth for me and provable in infinite ways as the truth. All of this will only become the truth for you when you begin this journey of yourself.

What has been expressed and will be expressed is just simply your road map with the necessary signs of direction to ensure you that your on the right road and headed in the right direction.

For a very small few, what has been said and will be said , will validate numerous things they've already experienced but just hadn't reached that point where it all began to materialize into words.

For those of you whom that fits, what has been said will feel natural like its been there waiting to come into focus within your conscious mind.

Just be not discouraged but rather encouraged because it's a long, sometimes difficult but beautiful journey that's worth it.

I'm only doing to you and for you that which was done to me and for me by numerous people.

Numerous people and experiences, where sometimes the very people who opened my mind and heart farther, didn't even realize what they were teaching me through my experiences with them while others engaged me sometimes in fierce but oh so positive and deep conversations that gave me indicators of being guided on the right path.

There are a few things that have been stated earlier in prior chapters that out of necessity must be stated again.

" Love is not a feeling or emotion although it facilitates both in the process of making itself known to the one or ones in whom love has become awakened "

" Love is a spiritual thing that isn't physical or material based but exists as the essence in and behind all that is physical and connected or unified. "

"Love isn't defined by nor confined by time, distance, circumstances, place , the presence of a person's body or the lack of a person's body.

Love escapes and defies the boundaries of all things to exist as the most powerful force by which all things are connected, grown, healed, and changed into the best results possible even when the odds of it seem too overwhelming to happen or become true. "

" The degree to which one learns to believe and trust in love unconditionally directly determines the degree of love's power to accomplish what it is meant to accomplish in the lives of human beings "

Love is an inner spiritual force of consciousness that has the power and ability to assimilate and supersede any and all dimensions of the mind's thought processes and redefine its underlying foundation until all thoughts ,feelings , perceptions .and attitudes are filtered through love's directives and made to bear the imprint of its influence.

An influence so powerful to the point of being able to give more vibrant radiance and in depth definition and purpose to things and people in the surrounding environment that previously seemed to hold no real aim, purpose, or meaning until seen again by the one or ones now able to see through the eyes of Love.

It is as well an inner force of divine magnetic properties consisting of a inner intelligent energy that emanates from the soulful essence of one's being, then on through the very mental fabric of thought as a means to implementing it's expressive and informative nature through channels of influence so that it may transcend from its internal (heart) position of existence within one person into the internal (heart) position of another person to seek expression and connection there so that it may or can seek to Aid in the awakening of another dimension of itself within the other person.

Where ,when or if combined, then truly grows, develops, and becomes nurtured into a greater and more Fuller degree of power and expression of itself within the connection with the other.

There is an alarming and very disturbing characteristic of thinking, perception, and feeling not only within modern times but in much of the past eras of time as well that has prevented love from truly being in the world on any significant or widespread level.

The alarming and disturbing characteristics of thinking, perceiving, and feeling that has done this is a continuum of dislike and disregard for the positive nature and positive aim, direction , and purpose of things like love that bring its own rules , principles, and requirements that must be complied with in order to be allowed to approach it , truly realize it, and experience it along with the fullest benefits and possibilities incorporated within the results that are produced only by the event of total compliance with the dictates of its nature.

People have been fond of quoting , giving an unlimited amount of speeches and writing enough volumes to fill 4 or 5 N.F.L. Football Stadiums about love in the Bible and what it means.

None of them has yet to give the true meaning of love as it is used in those (2) New Testament verses because of :

- The true nature and roots of that which surrounds the word love in the scriptures ,
- The nature of the hearts of the people today behind the interpretations and leadership with the Bible.

Historically, the true meaning wasn't conceivable because when they were written (2 Centuries after the time that Jesus or the Disciples supposedly lived) , the comprehension of them escaped their grasp because of the nature of their hearts and the intent for the Bible (Conquerings & forced conversions / Emperor Constantine + Council of Nicaea to formulate New Testament Scripture).

Romans Ch. 13 vs. 8 - " The one who has loved another has fulfilled the law "

Romans Ch. 13 vs. 10 - "Love is the fulfillment of law "

Why use those verses in this book ? How are they relevant? Just simply to prove a point about something .

The basis of one of love's most influential and most defining principles is something that people who like thinking wrong and doing wrong have a intense disregard for. (What is right).

How does that relate to love ? The basis of law is to influence and enforce what is right with penalties of punishment for the breaking of those laws. The fear of the punishment is meant to influence compliance to the law.

To fulfil the intent of the law means that one has grown to love the doing of right so much until they think and perform what is right not out of a desire for a reward or due to the fear of a punishment, they just simply do it unconditionally out of a love for right.

Everything else is to be considered and based upon an ulterior motive other than the right one.

So the point is that the basis of love is (RIGHT). The totality of what is right is The right thoughts, the right intentions, the right attitude, the right perceptions, and the right actions which consistently produces the right results as the nature of love intends and ensures.

The fruit of thinking and doing what is right to others is : fairness , justice, equality and healthy relationships. Something that the governments, Educational halls of learning, and the major religions of the world can't and won't do because they're all from the basis of a world order that was built upon wrong, thus a natural impediment and to love in the world.

CHAPTER 9

The Feminine & Masculine Essences : Love's Ultimate Connection Of Power

The Nature, Basis, & Dynamics Of Male-Female Relations

So what does all of this really mean? It means that the feminine and masculine essences each has a particular role and function to fulfill that is neither lesser or greater in regards to each other but rather individual pieces of a whole with their own natures designed to complement and complete each other in areas that one may have qualities better suited for things that the other doesn't possess to the extent or degree that the other does. One of those particular areas is physical strength which the ancients knew to be balanced by the fact that the feminine contributed to the essence of that which determines physical strength

Ultimately through the influences of her feminine nature is the main defining factor that brought moderation to the usages of man's physical strength and helped to keep

man's physical strength within boundaries of moderation.

The Foundational key & Lock To Human Progress Or Stagnation

The first comfort that

any man knows is that of a mother because the woman by nature is the ultimate comforter, balancer, moderator, developer, and the ultimate conceiver , thinker, and maintainer of essential things (especially an eye for details) and many more qualities of importance.

All of those principles of nature when properly perceived and connected to by man ,naturally translates into positive balanced causes and effects in every avenue of civilization.

The so-called female and her feminine essence is fulfilled, grown, and sustained continuously by mainly acknowledging, respecting, and connecting with the masculine essence in man in a complimentary role that helps produce harmony, balance ,peace, and growth between the two essences of feminine and masculine.

The man by nature is better suited for physical tasks of the enforcement and maintaining of the security of the household, society, and civilization as well as the implementation of his nature's propensities towards shaping, building, facilitating, directing , maintaining, and securing along with numerous other elements which also translates into relationships, household, society ,culture, and governing but in a way that acknowledges, respects, and connects with the feminine essence in a complimentary role that helps produce and sustain harmony, peace growth , and balance between the two essences of feminine and masculine in all areas of Civilization. Which means that no area of civilization could ever be truly healthy , balanced, or complete without the representation of equal participation and imparting from both Essences.

The dysfunction in the relationships , household, family structure, and society originates not only out of a lack knowledge and understanding of love but also from both men and women lacking a knowledge and understanding of their own individual essences and the roles dictated by them.

Today, many women out of necessity have had to take on roles of the male in the family and household structure due to the lack of a fatherly presence in the household and the children's lives because of incarcerated ,dead, or trifling fathers not fulfilling their responsibilities or roles and it's been that way so long until it's become a cultural norm for women to fulfill the functions of the male which becomes hard for women to switch back from even when some male appears in their lives because their efforts have been the only dependable force in their lives or their children's lives which has a dire consequence of influencing female children to think and believe that their mother's or grandmother's example is the only real choice and example to emulate.

The before mentioned examples and information were intended to cause both sides of the coin both feminine and masculine to rethink and reposition themselves into accordance with their nature so that the source of the dysfunctions can finally be addressed and begin to be taken through a healthy process of elimination within every human relation.

Strangely this is the representation of a process that many are not going to be willing to acknowledge, consider ,or even implement because of certain negative roles and expectations that both feminine and masculine beings have become entrenched within.

Most men feel that they not only want to believe but have to believe that the being we call woman is lesser than them in order for them to feel Superior and that the woman is best suited to be a plaything ,servant or subservient being to all that is male in the name of entertainment, fun ,and sex.

Equally, the majority of the incorrectly named feminine beings known as woman feels a want or need to remain in a negative passive role of being and doing that which gives credence to the male's disrespectful, condescending, and devaluing egotistical views of females and their perceived purposes for females of the same nature.

It is the lack of knowledge of self and one's true feminine nature that influences these ignorant choices of a self- inflicted confinement that prevents the majority of so-called females from even knowing and understanding how and why to have love for self.

Until this particular dysfunction and all of its elements are alleviated there will never be a universal demonstration and implementation of Love within male and female relationships to no great or significant extent.

This is about one having love within the context of their very nature and demonstrating it from that particular context because to do otherwise is to attempt to initiate and facilitate a false perceived notion of Love out of context and perpetuate the damage , disorder, and unnatural effects produced from this ignorance.

This is only a sample of what it means to go beyond the surface.

There are some regardless of what is said and how it is proven ,they will continue in the same course of thought ,belief , and action. This is the kind of person who should still be shown unconditional kindness , respect, and care because experience is the best teacher and it isn't up to us to determine when and how that person changes the course of their thinking , it one's duty to only plant the seeds of suggestive thought and direction then allow time and experience to produce the proper elements necessary for growth.

The realm of truth and love are unconditional but it is people's reactions that are conditional and based upon a desire to resist change because change has a way of leaving us naked , exposed , and in need of being redressed according to the dictates of a new idea and truth whose time has come.

There are four questions, one for the so-called females and the others for the male and all four are the most explosive and most indomitable questions to ever be implemented within the discussion of the dysfunctional Male- Female Relationships.

Questions within themselves that are so intense and forceful until no choice is left in one's mind except to rethink and begin to reevaluate the spectrum of ALL history dealing with the so-called female.

This question is for the so-called female :

"If modern man(of the past 5,000 + years) didn't historically treat you so-called females right, how can it ever be rational that he historically taught you right about yourself and taught the right knowledge of the so-called female?

None of this intended as an attack on the Black Male or belittling of the Black Male, it is only a means by which the Black Male must be forced to reexamine himself and the foreign unnatural standards of Manhood that have never served empower us but rather to entrap us into a design that benefits the Caucasian Male's progress in maintaining his dominance

By deception and the continued systematic strategy to alienate the Black Male from our true essence of self and its indomitable power that the world couldn't erase all signs of.

These questions are for the Male :

" **If modern man (of the past 5,000 + years) didn't historically treat the so-called female right , how could it ever be rational that he would teach the right things about her ,if his intent was to conquer others and even seek to redefine man according to new limitations of artificial value and positions that would only aid in enhancing and reinforcing a domination by a select few over all men through deception ? "**

Is it not a conquerors' nature to either destroy or disrupt the family dynamics of the Nation that has been conquered?

" What better way than to redefine both gender definition, potential ,and positions in a way that not only disrupts the cohesion of those nations but as well kills those conquered Nation's collective consciousness? "

The modern male ego is a very fragile thing that has been set up for complete failure and collapse when faced with facts that exist in a way that contradicts also everything man has ever thought and believed about himself.

To have to face something that seems to crumble one's whole psychological foundation under him is comparable to the withdrawal symptoms that drug addicts experiences when they are deprived of a drug that they're addicted to.

In the mind of the drug addict, it may be perceived as a unjust deprivation that hinders them from feeling good and alive but reality says the deprivation is good and healthy because its taking away some poison that's harming the drug addict.

Its the same with the Male whose addicted to a poisonous lie about Male superiority that's based upon the idea of a superiority to so-called females that's meant to be and justified by a standard of man's physical strength.

That false and exaggerated position of the modern Male ego is a poison that's implanted within the Black Male that has to be thrown away before the Black Male can even begin to see himself and properly align himself with the Black so-called female.

The So-called female manifests the essence of living things (the future people of a nation-) that the male with his strength and mastery of the physical material world guides and shapes in the world. The future generations.

As opposed to the definitional constructs of Western Civilization for the Male and female, they are in truth not and NEVER have been opposites or opposing elements of two different spectrums to be measured against each other in a unnatural standard of measurement to determine lesser and greater so that an unnatural conclusion of overall supremacy can be determined.

The (2) Essences (Male & Female)

The (2) essences are actually two components of the same unit that compliment each other and fit together by nature like a puzzle.

According to the dictates of Western Civilization and its Eurocentric cultural norms and standards. The (2) are genders that are to be defined and regulated according to the precepts of what was established in their collective ancestral history of Europe.

This particular Eurocentric model for interactions between what they call "Genders" has and will forever instigate and enforce inequalities and injustices between the two that will always favour the Male as the superior and the female as the inferior no matter what the Caucasian Male establishment does to influence the idea of them giving females equality and better treatment. It is always deception by another and another nice sounding name or policy.

How is that so? Because of one main principle that also applies to Black People (Including The Brown branch of The tree.)

No entity, establishment , or person can make or position another to be equal with it.

Equality is a state of mind with every necessary ability and capability to make itself equal by its own self-determination, self-preservation actions therein that are produced and sustained continuously by that one aspiring to equal another from a self- generating process of those things that make them equal to another.

To be told you're being treated equal or that you've been made equal is only a deceptive illusion when the source of that which is said to be making one equal originates from and is sustained by the other giving you equality or equal treatment.

Do the Caucasian have to continuously vote on whether they will remain the dominant race in all of their Caucasian ruled countries? No because that's not up for discussion. Does the Caucasian Male have to vote whether they'll give total control or access to the Caucasian female ir any other female? No because that's not up for consideration no matter how any individual females they (allow) to have certain high ranking positions.

Why? Because when you're truly equal, you don't have to petition anyone or conduct a vote for some permission to have something. You naturally have it already and don't need anyone's permission to do or use what is desired.

This is a process that applies to all human relations but in this context, it is applied specifically to so-called Female/Male Relationships.

At multiple stages in family relations ,friendships ,and relationships there's naturally going to be disagreements. Especially in the beginning.

Why?   because at the beginning, what you have is the meeting of different thoughts ,ideas ,opinions ,and perceptions about things between sometimes similar but different minds and personalities.

The more these seemingly different minds and personalities communicate and experience one another ,the more the differences lesson as familiarity reveals connecting points up on which two or more minds and personalities can merge together on common grounds within the things that previously seemed different and contrary on the surface.

As the communication process buds a unique Bond, the developing of affections and consideration for the other begins to take shape and become stronger.

When the affection grows, there is a natural repositioning that takes place within the mind and heart of each of the ones who have grown close.

That repositioning involves valuing and appreciating the other enough to put them and what they think, believe, or perceive before their own.

When both do this in reference to one another, a natural degree of compromise is produced between them.

At that point the means by which true communication can be established and maintained has occurred.

What does that further mean ? It means that the friction base and the extremities of irrational thinking and feeling within a disagreement is no longer existent within the connection between them. This doesn't mean that disagreement will no longer happen, it simply means that the friction and the extreme irrational point of arguing and fussing has been neutralized and replaced with the real and solid principles of unification such as respect, compromise, true consideration, and understanding for the other.

This is a highly matured and balanced degree that influences each to consider the other thoughts ,feelings ,and perceptions before their own in a deeper sense that redefines the communication process and the problem resolution process.

What does that mean? That means whenever there is a disagreement, there will always be the thought of compromise at the Forefront of the two's mind that will influence them to listen to each other and then take individual time to themselves where within their own thought processes, begin to analyse and measure ways to put the other's opinions and perceptions before theirs and figure out the way to combine the two individual thoughts or ideas into one method or one course of action for them to implement together.

This is the true unification process as a result of a true communication process based upon the affections or love that exists between them. It is the direct result of keeping the proper perspective while dealing with the struggles of experience so that the outcome is positive and conducive to strengthening the connection between two people.

The Principal Feminine Essence

The principle of femininity, often associated with qualities such as nurturing, creation, and balance, can be observed and validated consistently throughout nature and the universe.

This principle of femininity is not limited to the human or animal species but transcends into an illimitable array of natural processes, biological systems, and even phenomena of the universe's very fabric of existence.

By analysing these aspects, we can gain a deeper understanding of how femininity permeates the fabric of existence itself everywhere.

In nature, femininity is prominently displayed and showcased in the reproductive processes of most living organisms.

Female organisms are often an unequivocal component essential to the process of creation, the of nurturing new life , and the natural systems that facilitate them all.

Example :

In many species, the female's role in childbirth is critical. This process is not only a significant biological function but also a principal nurturing act, where mothers provide care, protection, and sustenance to their babies.

This maternal principle of instinct ensures the survival and continuation of species, emphasizing the importance and high necessity of feminine principles in the natural world.

Beyond the scope of individual organisms, ecosystems also exhibit feminine qualities through their innate balance and interdependence. Ecosystems thrive on cooperation and the delicate equilibrium between various species and their environments.

That balance is a direct image of and intricate sister of the nurturing and harmonious aspects of femininity.

Example :

The delicate but highly efficient symbiotic relationships between pollinators and plant life such as bees, demonstrate a mutual nurturing that structuralizes , supports , and ensures the health and vitality of entire ecosystems.

Those highly organized interactions are essential to the reproduction of plants and the survival of pollinating species.

That is a demonstration of the pervasive power and influence of feminine principles in nature's interconnected spectrum of life.

In the sphere of plants, femininity can be observed in the reproductive structures and processes that sustain life across numerous spheres of life for plants and humans alike.

Although plants possess both male and female reproductive organs, it is often the female part, the ovary, that develops into fruit thus providing new seeds for the next generation of its kind.

This cycle of growth, reproduction, and nurturing new life not only mirrors the human so-called female but is actually directly connected and aligned with her through that feminine principle of energy so that none has ever equalled the so-called female in not only growing plant life but also understanding every use of plant life for medicines and vitamins until so- called female was most equipped to be the original doctors of the ancient world.

That amongst other understandings of the ancients is why the question of the so-called female's equality was never in doubt or up for a vote and why the penalty was unquestionably death for disrespecting the so-called female.

The principle of femininity extends vastly beyond even all of that into geological and scales of the universe. The Earth itself is often personified as a nurturing mother, providing resources, sustenance, and shelter to all forms of life.

That view is validated in various cultural mythologies and scientific understandings of the Earth as a self-regulating system, often referred to as the Gaia hypothesis. This concept suggests that the Earth functions as a single organism, with its various components working in harmony to maintain the conditions necessary for life, exactly like a mother tending to her offspring.

On a larger and more powerful scale, the universe exhibits feminine principles throughout the processes of creation and destruction that drive its development. Stars, often referred to as the "nurseries" of the universe, play a crucial role in the creation of elements and the formation of planets and galaxies.

The very birth of stars themselves from clouds of gas and dust, their life cycles, and eventual demise in supernovas contribute to the ongoing creation and transformation of the universe.

That continuous cycle of creation, nurturing, and renewal is a reflection of the feminine principles at the deepest and most powerful level of any scale of measurement.

Furthermore, the existence of dark matter and dark energy in the universe can be directly linked to feminine principles.

Those mysterious but real and largely unseen forces are thought to constitute the majority of the universe's mass and energy, governing the structure and expansion of the universe.

The nurturing and guiding roles designated specifically to dark matter and dark energy resonate with the unseen but pervasive influence primarily equated with femininity.

In conclusion, the principle of femininity is so intricately embedded into the fabric of nature and the universe.

From the reproductive processes of individual organisms to the balance and interdependence of ecosystems, and from the nurturing Earth to the cycles of the universe and the process of creation, femininity plays a crucial and Unequalled part in the perpetuation and harmony of life.

The most hidden truth in her regard is the fullness of the so-called female's identity and power that connects the so-called female to the Unequalled feminine energy throughout the universe and directly from The Creator of whom she is a direct part of.

Understanding these principles of Unequalled power and influence should not only escalate and solidify our appreciation of femininity's profound universal impact and significance beyond cultural and human contexts but it should as well cause a redefining of how we perceive and approach the so-called female.

Throughout all that has been expressed and valudated by the natural and principal workings of femininity in nature and the universe, a pattern developed that showed us Numerous (but not all) principles of femininity that are in of themselves prerequisites to any family, community ,society, government, and civilization that is to be just, nurturing, and positive.

Undeniably, what was also shown and validated was one central theme if the feminine nature's natural and unequivocal propensity to produce, sustain, and advance the core of all primary systems.

So it should no longer be a mystery why or how the feminine nature excels at mathematics and the principle dynamics of science more so than the masculine essence.

How could anyone ever degrade , disrespect, and devalue one such as her unless they're truly sociopathic and barbaric by nature and from cultural proclivities that reflect the same nature?

Until relationships are realized, known, and understood in their proper context and nature as a natural system based upon the feminine and masculine essences being in their proper positions and contexts in relations to their individual selves and each other, the dysfunctions will continue.

Most females and males perceive relationships as genies in a bottle that just pop up naturally as expected or desired and perform according to a natural pattern by its own accord . As if no right knowledge of the process is required on order to produce and main the results.

To the average female in current times and even in the past times being female mint and basically means today simply having children, relationships with men ,laying on your back having sex ,flirting ,being sexy ,and that is about the extent of it.

There is the predominant thought that being female is all about the moment, all about the era in which one lives, all about the activities that one experiences as an individual female while the individual female lives.

Never realizing that the feminine aspect is more about that which is transmitted into the later generations of the female.

Just because you no longer are able to have children does not nullify the continuance or activation of you being female on another level.

It just means that you can no longer demonstrate the principles of your femininity on one level and that is meant to be so by nature but that doesn't nullify the existence of other levels and other responsibilities that one's femininity dictates.

In the ancient times of news numerous civilizations of black people are people of dog skin origins there was the existence of teachings and schools by females that was passed down from female to female so much so until in some civilizations such as Egypt and Sumerian there was particular schools that was specifically for the female so that the principles of femininity could easily could be taught, implemented ,and passed to later female generations.

This was a particular established systematic continuation of the proper demonstration and expression of the proper feminine principles of power from one feminine generation to the next.

Within that system, the females even had their own language called : Eme - Sal dialect.

What does that mean ? It means that grandmotherhood has duties and obligations of femininity to their Children that birthed their grandchildren and to the female grandchildren to help reinforce and advance the feminine principles according to their frightful nature.

This idea makes the average female cringe with dislike and disagreement because grandmotherhood is their retirement plan. Why ? How could any female feel that way ? Because of a lack of true love and appreciation for their Feminine essence and nature.

The Principal Masculine Essence

"Until the dark skin man or man of dark skin origins has gone searching into the depths of his inner self that has repeatedly failed him, trapped him, and misled him. Only then will he discover and overcome his worst enemies that lurk in the shadows of his mind's ignorance as another man's deceptive implant of inferiority. "

"The Black man will only become qualified and ready to truly become a cornerstone and leader of his family and race , only after he's succeeded in finding and redefining himself under the command and Leadership of his own true nature and the power of True love, purpose, discipline, poise ,and intelligence that it provides. "

"Very few are taught by the instructive word instead most people in the world have to be taught by affliction because many are hard-headed and are only forced to learn the hardest of lessons that would otherwise be easy if not for the power of stubbornness that is the twin of ignorance."

"There is just something life-changing about the event of having been under the constant fire of affliction's massive weapons that inevitably forces and leads a man from weakness of mind into the strength of a new found consciousness by the stress of bitter experiences. "

(Discipline & A System Of Regularity)

"There can be no permanence of success or permanence of change from a negative counterproductive mentality without a love of discipline and regularity. "

"The nature of a system is a construct kf elements in a reoccurring sequence that renders chaos, confusion, and disorder no longer possible "

'The unsystematic mind is an imbalanced and undisciplined mind that will never be able to compare to or approach efficiency, speed, and rate of accuracy (aka Success) of another man of a systematic mind.

" Most people who dislikes and rejects discipline and order, have minds driven by carelessness, inconsistent patterns of thought and action, and frivolous pursuits."

**" Until the Black man / Male of Dark skin
origins learns to appreciate and love the
workings of a mental and physical system for his
own life, he ,his family, and race will forever be
ruled, regulated, and confined by another man's
system."**

When it comes to the black man's perceived masculinity and manhood, there are some major questions that have yet to be asked like : Whose model or standard or we using to measure and determine what those things are ?, What they mean ?, and How those particular things function ?

As with anything in order for one to gain a proper perspective of things one must have a starting point and a destination.

Each of those is a particular context through which one must be able to properly perceive one's position and condition of mind ,

Within this particular venture as with any particular venture or thing that one has under study, there must be a starting point and a destination.

Within this particular Venture the starting point is of a dual nature.

- **The present tense of time**
- **The origins of one's kind**

Each is to be analysed and weighed at different times and stages In the course of the examination and analysis.

The present tense of time is to gain a grass up on not only one's true mentality position in life but as well as ones true position in reference to everything else in his environment.

The origin tense is the standard of measurement that the present tense will be compared to in order to determine the points of compliance with the principles of the original model, points of deviation from the original model's principles of existence and wealth and exactly whether the current model is right or wrong.

Masculinity, shaped by cultural norms, varies significantly between European and African/Asian standards, often emphasizing conflicting ideals.

In European contexts, masculinity has historically emphasized traits like aggression, violence, dominance, deceptiveness , and a desire to misalign things from their natural order.

At numerous historical points of the past, the Eurocentric standards of masculinity meant that before a boy could attain Manhood, the ultimate degree of masculinity, he had to engage in anal and oral sex with his educational and war training masters. This was common in Sparta, Greece, Rome, Crete, and amongst the cultural norms of the Mycenaean (Mainland Greece 1600 BCE -1100 BCE)

This model often ties masculinity to economic success and leadership roles, fostering a sense of individualism and a lack of emotional restraints.

Conversely, African and Asian concepts of masculinity from their ancient cultural practices, although numerous, all had common principles that frequently prioritized community values, emphasizing family duty, respect for elders, Justice , respect & fairness to females, and interconnectedness within the community.

These ideals often challenge Western notions as they always have by valuing emotional expressiveness, cooperation, and nurturing roles alongside traditional expectations of strength and provider roles.

Furthermore, European masculinity is often tied to colonial histories and patriarchal structures that reinforced dominance and control.

 In contrast, African and Asian masculinities are influenced by diverse cultural and religious beliefs, incorporating spiritual dimensions and roles that go beyond economic provider or warrior ideals.

The differences also manifest in societal expectations: European masculinity tends to reinforce hierarchies where men exclusively dominate public spheres , while African and Asian ideals historically emphasized harmony and balance between genders that historically expressed itself in co-operative dual leadership in government, culture and society with the female.

After the European Colonization of much of Africa and Asia, only then did these norms of masculinity change significantly for the African/ Asian cultures.

What does all of that mean? It simply means that the mass majority of Black Men and those of Black origins in America and wherever else they are found in the world, have adapted the masculine standards and concepts of the very Caucasian Male establishment whose very Masculinity has never served him or others well.

This should naturally resonate as one of the main sources of the Black Male's negative contribution to the dysfunctions in the Black Male/Female relationship dynamic.

This assimilation into Caucasian Masculine standards has become culturalized in numerous veins of Black culture and you don't have to go far to see it or hear it.

The Systematic Element Of Masculinity

Everything in the universe, world ,and nature operate on principles of systematic order that are highly efficient and successful in their functioning.

This efficiency can be observed in various natural processes and ecosystems, where every component plays a crucial role in maintaining balance and sustainability. One main example: The systematic efficiency of the water cycle.

The process of evaporation, condensation, and precipitation ensures that water is continuously recycled and distributed across the planet. This cycle supports life by providing fresh water to ecosystems and regulating climate patterns. The water cycle's ability to sustain itself without external influence or assistance emphasizes nature's inherent efficiency.

In a similar way , the food chain demonstrates nature's systematic organization.

Producers, such as plants, receive and convert solar energy into food through photosynthesis. The Herbivores (Animals) consume these plants, and in turn, become food for carnivores and omnivores animals and humans.

Decomposers like fungi and bacteria break down dead organisms, returning nutrients to the soil. This intricate chain ensures energy flow and nutrient cycling, maintaining ecosystem health.

Each organism's role is vital, and their interactions create a balanced and self-regulating system.

Natural selection is another fundamental principle that drives the efficiency of biological systems.

Through the process of evolution, species adapt to their environments, developing traits that enhance their survival and reproduction. This results in organisms that are highly specialized and efficient in their niches.

Human systems, such as economies and social structures, also draw inspiration from natural principles of efficiency and sustainability.

The one structure in nature that is yet to act in accordance with true positive principles of systematic order is human relationships.

Why ? because all else in nature thinks, acts, and performs naturally and consistently in sync with its nature while humans continue to think, act, and function against the grain of their nature producing all dysfunctions.

Relationships are in essence meant to be a system of relating that produces positive results.

For example :

Circular economies aim to imitate nature's recycling processes, reducing waste and making the most of available resources.

By studying and applying these principles, humans can create systems that are more positive, natural, sustainable and efficient.

The natural world operates on principles of systems that are inherently efficient and successful.

Those systematic principles ensure the sustainability and balance of ecosystems, demonstrating the incredible adaptability and optimization of life on Earth.

Understanding and emulating these principles can guide human endeavors into a more efficient and frictionless nature.

Everything in the universe, world ,and nature operate on principles of systematic order that are highly efficient and successful in their functioning.

This efficiency can be observed in various natural processes and ecosystems, where every component plays a crucial role in maintaining balance and sustainability.

One main example: The systematic efficiency of the water cycle.

The process of evaporation, condensation, and precipitation ensures that water is continuously recycled and distributed across the planet. This cycle supports life by providing fresh water to ecosystems and regulating climate patterns.

The water cycle's ability to sustain itself without external influence or assistance emphasizes nature's inherent efficiency.

In a similar way , the food chain demonstrates nature's systematic organization.

Producers, such as plants, receive and convert solar energy into food through photosynthesis. The Herbivores (Animals) consume these plants, and in turn, become food for carnivores and omnivores animals and humans.

Decomposers like fungi and bacteria break down dead organisms, returning nutrients to the soil. This intricate chain ensures energy flow and nutrient cycling, maintaining ecosystem health.

Each organism's role is vital, and their interactions create a balanced and self-regulating system.

Natural selection is another fundamental principle that drives the efficiency of biological systems.

Through the process of evolution, species adapt to their environments, developing traits that enhance their survival and reproduction. This results in organisms that are highly specialized and efficient in their niches.

Human systems, such as economies and social structures, also draw inspiration from natural principles of efficiency and sustainability.

The one structure in nature that is yet to act in accordance with true positive principles of systematic order is human relationships.

Why ? because all else in nature thinks, acts, and performs naturally and consistently in sync with its nature while humans continue to think, act, and function against the grain of their nature producing all dysfunctions.

Relationships are in essence meant to be a system of relating that produces positive results.

For instance, circular economies aim to imitate nature's recycling processes, reducing waste and making the most of available resources.

By studying and applying these principles, humans can create systems that are more positive, natural, sustainable and efficient.

In conclusion, the natural world operates on principles of systems that are inherently efficient and successful. These principles ensure the sustainability and balance of ecosystems, demonstrating the incredible adaptability and optimization of life on Earth.

Understanding and emulating these principles can guide human endeavors toward greater efficiency and sustainability.

Human systems, such as economies and social structures, also draw inspiration from natural principles of efficiency and sustainability.

For instance : Circular economies aim to mimic nature's recycling processes, reducing waste and making the most of available resources.

By studying and applying these principles, humans can create systems that are more sustainable and non - counterproductive.

Systematic thinkers tend to be more efficient, successful, and regular in their actions as opposed to unsystematic thinkers.

Why ? because they approach tasks with structured planning and clear strategies, leading to consistent and predictable outcomes. They prioritize, organize, and manage their time effectively, reducing wasted effort and enhancing productivity. By anticipating challenges and creating contingency plans, they can navigate obstacles smoothly.

In contrast, unsystematic thinkers often act impulsively, leading to inconsistency and inefficiency. Their lack of organization can result in missed opportunities and repeated mistakes.

This is especially seen in Male/Female Relationships. Overall, systematic thinking fosters disciplined, goal-oriented behavior, driving greater success and reliability.

Self-discipline means the ability to control one's impulses, emotions, and behaviors to achieve long-term goals.

It involves consistently making choices that align with one's values and objectives more so than an occupation with trifling desires, even when faced with distractions or challenges.

This trait enables individuals to stay focused, work diligently, and overcome obstacles, leading to personal growth and success.

Human systems, such as economies and social structures, also draw inspiration from natural principles of efficiency and sustainability. For instance, circular economies aim to mimic nature's recycling processes, reducing waste and making the most of available resources. By studying and applying these principles, humans can create systems that are more sustainable and non - counterproductive.

Systematic thinkers tend to be more efficient, successful, and regular in their actions as opposed to unsystematic thinkers.

Why ? because they approach tasks with structured planning and clear strategies, leading to consistent and predictable outcomes. They prioritize, organize, and manage their time effectively, reducing wasted effort and enhancing productivity. By anticipating challenges and creating contingency plans, they can navigate obstacles smoothly.

In contrast, unsystematic thinkers often act impulsively, leading to inconsistency and inefficiency. Their lack of organization can result in missed opportunities and repeated mistakes. This is especially seen in Male/Female Relationships.

Overall, systematic thinking fosters disciplined, goal-oriented behavior, driving greater success and reliability.

Self-discipline means the ability to control one's impulses, emotions, and behaviors to achieve long-term goals.

It involves consistently making choices that align with one's values and objectives more so than an occupation with trifling desires, even when faced with distractions or challenges.

This trait enables individuals to stay focused, work diligently, and overcome obstacles, leading to personal growth and success.

When it comes to manhood ,most young guys are even grown men have thought for years that being a grown man or being masculine meant that you can just wake up one day and decide that you're a man and that you can go forth to just deal with the world according to your own thoughts, standards, beliefs ,and perceptions and the world would to just fall in compliance with whatever was conceived.

Time and time again this particular mentality was forced not only to recognize another reality but was forced to act in accordance with the other reality that was dictated by someone else.

Someone else that was able to not only out maneuver them but basically out think them and strategically place or maneuver them into positions in society, government, and even their own family structure that was desired and designed by the other people who have been out thinking them.

Most Young males think that masculinity and being a man is something easy to do or acquire.

The young males today even have that microwave popcorn attitude and perception that manhood and masculinity is something Instant without any particular work or requirements being involved or any particular sacrifices being involved.

The sad thing is that many have known for over 20 to 30 years that there's a vicious cycle that's been implanted within the black community and the black family structure to facilitate the elimination of the male and manhood element from the black family structure.

This was done so in order to disable that male and manhood element and disable any means by which a significant amount of younger guys could actually come into the knowledge understanding and strategic part of what Black manhood actually is and still must become.

Where's the young Male's getting their ideas and understanding about manhood and masculinity from ?

One source is from a significant amount of Older B li ack males who never a clue themselves but made but made it up.

The other is the power in the world and the one who dictates policy, meaning, and position to the whole world either by the threat of violence or by actual violence that keeps even the Black rich, religious , or even politician in fear, in check and bowed.

How is that possible? Because the male youth practice it everyday on themselves in urban gang warfare or other violent acts based upon an idea to control certain areas as territory for exclusive drug sales markets.

This culture of violence has a higher tendency toward disrupting or destroying family structures as most end up incarcerated and next highest percentage end up dead.

Gangsters, shooters and killers are the titles most valued in that culture. Who originally possessed and popularized those titles? Find the answer and you'll also discover who they are truly following.

The Original Man : Follower Or Trend Setter ?

The first and foremost principal that has to be established is who the original man is.

It is a scientifically biological fact that no dark Skin people can in any shape, form, or fashion descend from a pale skin people.

Why and How ? because pale skin, blue eyes, and ,blonde hair are biologically assigned the lease, lowest ,and impossible common denominator with originating anything within the biological genetic makeup of the human species other than that which is established within it.

Why or how because dark skin rests upon the same principle of existence as darkness from which it came.

Darkness is not a color as black is not a color. They are both exclusively primary points of origin which things derive or evolve from such as color.

It's simple, although highly detested facts that light cannot produce or even imitate the power and potential of darkness, that light originates from darkness and the source of light's energy is found only within darkness so therefore the livelihood and energy base on which light depends, originates from darkness therefore making light dependant upon darkness for its very existence. This is an indomitable principle of the universe that is manifest within many realms of the universe and the Earth as well.

Darkness is often perceived incorrectly as a void or a symbol of negativity. The negativity attached to darkness and its equivalent, Black or Blackness, has its origins within psychological mind frames and cultural tenets of Caucasians who very origins have a basis in periods of ignorance where the level of civilization for them was minute or non-existent.

There are two such periods in Caucasian history.

1. The Caucasoid pre-civilization era where they were confined to the mountainous region of the Caucasus Mountains from which their race name originates. That era of the cavemen is called the first Dark Age.

2. The time of the 900 -mid……….when the Black Moors brought Civilization back to Europe after is total collapse.

Contrary to those negative cultural myths and customs of Caucasians,

Darkness is a fundamental principle of life, regeneration, and growth, both in the universe and on Earth.

Darkness plays a critical but exclusive role in numerous primary natural processes, illustrating its indispensable nature.

In the vast expanse of the universe, darkness is more than the absence of light; it is the foundation upon which the whole universe is constructed and sustained.

The universe primarily consists of dark matter and dark energy, which together make up about ninety-nine percent of the universe's total mass-energy content.

These dark components are essential for the structure and expansion of the universe. Dark matter acts as a gravitational web that holds galaxies together, preventing them from disintegrating.

Without the presence of dark matter, the visible matter that makes up stars and planets would not coalesce into galaxies, making the formation of life as we know it impossible.

Similarly, dark energy drives the accelerated expansion of the universe, ensuring that it continues to evolve and provide the conditions necessary for new stars and planetary systems to form.

On Earth, darkness is integral to the natural cycles that govern life. The most evident example is the diurnal cycle of day and night. Darkness, or night-time, allows for the processes of rest and regeneration. For many organisms, darkness triggers essential biological functions.

Humans and other animals rely on the absence of light to regulate their circadian rhythms through the production of melatonin, a hormone that induces sleep. This rest period is crucial for physiological repair, cognitive function, and overall health.

Without the restorative effects of darkness, the balance of these natural rhythms would be disrupted, leading to detrimental health effects.

In the plant kingdom, darkness is equally vital. While photosynthesis occurs during daylight, plants also undergo important processes in the dark.

For instance, respiration, where plants convert sugars into energy, predominantly happens at night. This process is essential for plant growth and development.

Additionally, All seeds require darkness to germinate, demonstrating that darkness is a catalyst for the initiation of life. Moreover, the absence of light helps regulate the photoperiodic responses of plants, influencing their flowering and fruiting cycles. Thus, darkness plays a direct role in the reproductive and growth phases of plant life.

Okay, what was the overall point and relevancy of that? It was the presentation of foundational principles of existence that define the basis of everything in the universe so that the ultimate definition and power of the origins of our dark skin could be realized , understood, and cemented into a better consciousness of what that implies and requires of us outside of any definitions , boundaries, or expectations that any non Black person or people may present to any of us.

The Ultimate point as well is to give keys to every creation epic ever formulated by our ancestors and to reveal its ever present purpose.

If you only look at those Creation Epics from one or a few dimensions of perception, you'll ALWAYS miss the truest forms of what is being displayed and expressed. Why? Or How ? Because their aim , purpose, and function was designed from an infinite mind and understanding of what we think of as The Creator or Supreme Being.

The Most powerful defining principle of approach, guiding thought , and perception is that :

"It is impossible to think or intend just one thought, One thought naturally insinuates or brings others into existence that are just as powerful and valid as the first"

Within everyone one of those Epic Creation Stories is the basis of everything in creation and their proper principles of nature, function, and results better known as Principles of Existence.

The keys to them ALL rests upon the degree to which you think, believe, and perceive in accordance with right and truth.

They were designed and encoded that way as natural defence mechanisms against any of impure thought and intent. Whether you believe that or not is inconsequential to the overall impact, influence, and power of thought and understanding that it provides.

Chapter 11 will be just a small demonstration of what those Epic Creations offer along with portions of ancient writings that the Caucasians have long sought after. To the point of having torn up Egypt and Nubia looking for them.

CHAPTER 10

Tough Love : Retribution

Today there is a generation divide and all of the black communities which includes the Puerto Rican Mexican and other black Latinos of Cuba South Central America Africa and the Polynesian Islands and other places.

The older Generations from the 1950 through 1982 have been looking at you today shaking their heads and other dislike complaining and seeing how pitiful and crazy they are.

The questions these older Generations deliberately fail to address is, who produced today's generation or the proud ones from 1972 through 1990 ? (Who were considered out of control crazy hard-headed and inattentive to the advice and instructions of the older people.)

Who influenced them to be that way? What is the youth's rebellion against the older generations, a sign of?

Older generations delude themselves and try to exonerate themselves from the blame by saying we taught them better than that, we raised them differently from that, or my children don't act like that, those are the children of those other kind of people black who didn't know how to raise their children as if them producing the next generations of uncaring and sell-out houseniggaz was the greatest thing since paved roads.

The hard truth is that the past four generations of Youth especially the males have been in Rebellion against the older Generations because the older Generations were and are still submissive in compliance and in worship of the forces of influence and people who have always unapologetically mistreated dark skin people.

The youth watch the older generations and wondered how they could be so slave like and fearful and basically made up their minds that they wouldn't think believe or act like the older generations.

To the old Generations those very thoughts and perceptions of them are misleading wrong or don't apply to them.

There's a small insignificant educated group of the older generations who have never cared about the conditions of their own people and you will find them as for removed from black communities as the Caucasians they've been living near or in the neighborhoods with as if they have escaped the reality of being black.

The youth saw that as well and began in the to 1970s to organize their own real family structures called gangs as a direct response to older generations' fake love ,fake family values , and faith beliefs.

It is still the same today for the same exact reasons but a little worse and today's generation are a continuum of the effects from the dysfunctions in the black family structure and relationships that originated from the older generations.

When the truth is told, we as a people are still going through the effects of the older generations and the sad thing about that is there is a significant amount of black people in whom the ideologies beliefs and feelings have been transmitted into the younger generations and thus made the conditions of black people in America and throughout the world worser and worser with each passing generation.

The youth many generations ago as the Youth of the present generation saw a divide between the older generations whereas you had a predominantly larger group of the older generation who were submissive and uncaring about the unjust and dangerous conditions perpetrated up on the black community by the descendants of past oppressors.

This significantly large portion of the black community was at odds with the smaller element of the black community that was willing to arm themselves and attempt to fight back not only did they dislike this small segment of the black community at times they was even willing to help the oppressors against this small element snitching them out ,turning them in and reporting on them.

The youth at that time even saw this and this became another of the motivating reasons of why they started forming gangs.

When you really think about it and the element of the older Generations that did this (as you have a significant amount of the current generation who thinks and acts this particular way), this is a deeply disturbing mentality that defies any logic and goes against any principal of loving ones people because the motivating thought is that "those particular type of people are going to mess it up for the rest of us who are trying to be good and obedient."

One would have to ask themselves is this in any shape form of fashion the appropriate State quality and condition of a older General? And when the particular question is answered correctly by a precise analyzation and comparison with the ancient precedents of how a population of people thought and reacted to external threats and dangers what one will see is a major difference.

Another sad element of the older Generations is that the history the standard history that they have accumulated talk and facilitated is a brand of history that is self-defeating and self-destructive in nature towards any future generations of black people because the nature of the history that is facilitated by them and will continue to be facilitated by them is a history that shows and encourages black Minds to assimilate themselves into systematic structures of those who have always disliked and oppressed black people for the expressed advancement of those people.

A history that is full of examples of what black people have contributed to Western civilization which on the surface would seem like the most positive example ever to be given but reality dictates that it is the most disrespectful self demeaning form of History to be implemented and facilitated by any people in the world that have been through the things that black people have been through.

Why is that so? mainly because the idea and intent of organizing these black Minds to make a contribution to the advancement of their own people has never come in to mind.

It's a fact that black people both male and female has contributed much on every level of Western civilization and they should be applauded because it shows the potential of the mind and capabilities of black minds but it does not influence and encourage the most important element of any mind towards his people which is to contribute their thoughts and resources of their thinking and capabilities for the advancement of their own people.

That is what people do and encourage when they are in direct according with the nature of who they are and live themselves and their people but this happens in opposite ways and contrary to the nature of who they are when the predominant thought behind education and learning is to continue to be a component of advancement for other people.

Even today black people have worked on space shuttles satellites aerial drones but at no time even with all the millionaires and a few billionaires in the world have any of them ever thought one time what about black people finally designing and constructing their own space shuttle and their own satellites so that they may become a power in this world that can directly influence the minds of their people from one generation to the next without ever again having to beg for permission or consideration for t.v .channels ,communication, services and the one area that is denied black people.... Satellite defense capabilities of other people who have never had the best interests of black people at heart.

Sadly the next penetrative question that gets to the heart of the matter is :What was and is the origin of the counterproductive substance of thinking and acting that drove the older generations?

The standard answer has always been a slave mentality carried over from slavery but that is only a small minute of the substance.

The complete shape and form of that substance goes back even into ancient times when at a particular point the civilizations of our people and those who had strayed away from civilization and began to implement frivolous and irrational practices and customs outside of the realm of reality and lost grip on the ultimate lessons and purpose of history.

History is not only the voice and guidance of a people from the past it is as well the one influential principle that allows and encourages the Improvement and advancement of principles from the past so that the future will be one of advancement as well.

The underlining intent and purpose of History has never been and never will be to pattern oneself after the full spectrum of that which is in the past because for one or a people to fashion themselves after everything in the particular past is to fashion themselves after the defects, problems, and limitations that allowed the ancestors of the past to be conquered in the first place.

There are those who try to interpret the event of slavery having happening in Africa and other parts of the world as if the people were just out thought and out maneuvered by a superior Force, when in fact if you look into what is left of those particular histories you will see that it was a universal decline in those civilizations and what was taught in those civilizations because at that particular point they could not advance that which they knew and understood which rests as the main reason why they were conquered and enslaved.

Ultimately identity and the substance of the identity within the people who qualify for the identity is meant to advance constantly from one stage and one period in time to the next in a continuous flow where the basis of the identity remains the same but the knowledge, understanding ,and power of the identity and the possibility that it creates continues to grow and advance.

No matter what it said there is no way possible for any particular person of black descent to accumulate or have access to any significant portion of those ancient civilizations and be able to construct a adequate and sufficient dynamics of iidentity.

Why? because it was either destroyed or wasn't written down and therefore is not available and to present a platform of putting together pieces of this and pieces of that is an incomplete stage that could never present the full identity and capability of those civilizations.

History is there the teachers the realm of possibility and to teach us a base of understanding and perception about the realm of possibility and impossibility about things that have historically been around our people and continue to be around our people and this is one of the most significant parts of history that has been underrated, ignored ,and denied.

A serious course of action that has resulted in a disorientation of mind and behavior when it comes to being able to properly perceive and respond to things and people according to the consistent reference frame of thought and actions that are not only in the present but are also well established in the past.

It is this standard of measurement that we have lacked and been naturally positioned to keep hoping and expecting things to be different or to possess the possibility of being different.

A thought and expectation point that has always been outside of the realm of reality as a continuous catalyst setting us up for failure and misperceiving the whole of reality around us and the people involved.

Out of necessity, an indomitable scale of measurement was formulated from the principle actions of ALL historical time periods to challenge and shatter present minds, philosophies, and beliefs about Caucasian People and their stance towards non Caucasian people.

It is : The Annihilator Scale.

The apex of measurement through which self-preservation and self-determination can only become a reality for Black People throughout the world.

[Gangstaz, Thugz, & Outlawz]

None of the previous things that have been said were in any shape, form ,or fashion a justification for gang violence and the senseless mentalities and deaths it continues to cause.

When you look at the essential mentality that exists within the game structure what you have is an acute case of cowardice, manipulation, and a lack of true love.

When you go back to the origins of the major game structures and the branches that have evolved from it since it's Origins, what you have is a hierarchy of ignorance motivated for selfish ulterior motives to use and discard others after they've outlived their purpose.

This is a fact that may anger many amongst the game Empire but it does not lessen the intensity of the truth that has been spoken.

It may be said how do you prove this when we are willing to die for each other?, when we are willing to die for the territory that we claim?, or when we are willing and ready to ride or die in an opps. against any and all that disrespect us or challenge us?

Well that is true to an extent, a very large extent that surprisingly includes those Within the same neighborhoods or similar neighborhoods that contain gang members but it does not apply in any shape form or fashion to the establishments around all of these game Turfs such as the police call any other law enforcement agency and their members.

There is a severe embedded fear of these establishments until just one or two of them of the character of Barney fight can show up with a six shot revolver and make the toughest meanest iron biting gang member or gang members drop everything that they have guns dopes and run.

Not just that but there are innumerable cases where the law enforcement agencies have shot down and killed members of these games and not one retaliation was put on the table against the ones who shot and killed one of their own members.

As a matter of fact the idea was bored from being conceived in the mind of the gang members due to this fear and explicit knowledge of the consequences that would be issued out if such an act of retaliation was to be carried out.

This is the evidence that you may have been questioning about.

This evidence in and of itself reveals the element of cowardice within the game establishment.

What else does this reveal? It also reveals that these games and gang members who promote themselves as being the ultimate killers aren't what they claim to be and that they are only killers to the ones that they know they have a high probability of getting away with it without any particular massive retaliation against them which is people of their own community or people of other poor communities.

Let's ask a high-powered question that none can duck or avoid, as a so-called killer how do you compare or measure up to the actual real killers of the world? How do you measure up to the real one shot killers who actually shoot from hundreds of yards away with one shot and one kill as the result?

The answer is quite easy. The gang members don't even come close to comparison or imitation of these real killers that exist outside of the games and the Gang membership.

How come that be said when they kill a lot of people when they shoot a lot of people?

That can be easy to say and proven by the mere fact that the average gang member doesn't even know how to accurately aim shoot and kill that which they are targeting.

It is proven by the fact that most of them favor automatic rifles because of the nature of the automatic rifle to release multiple rounds because in actuality they can't aim; it takes multiple rounds for them to even get close to hitting their mark. Where most of the time they end up hitting shirt sleeves, pants legs, fingernails, part of a hairdo, a light pole that was next to the Target, or a car that was next to the Target.

So does this sound like a real killer? Someone who actually knows how to use the tool of a firearm or automatic weapon??

Major principles of these games sometimes is symbols that have points to them that are supposed to represent different things but especially represent love, but when you really get down to it ,not one of the original founders of these gangs or current head gang leaders of these gangs actually know what love is and this actually leads and facilitate these gangs in ways that actually are counterproductive to what love is actually about.

If you were to ask any one of those gang leaders or gang founders about what love is ,not a single one of them would be able to define it for you and according to that which they say they represent which is love for that particular gang and the laws and philosophy there in, then by the fact of not knowing what love actually is, this disqualifies them from being in those leadership roles because they cannot teach that which they do not know.

If you are a gang member within a certain gang that believes in the principle of love but you have a leadership that does not know what love is, how is it that they can teach you love for that which you are supposed to be representing or beginning to learn to represent when they don't know what love is?

Going even farther, if you call yourself a soldier within one of these gang structures and your level of soldiering is at the level with Boy Scouts when compared to real killers, then there is something wrong with where you're at and the leadership there in if they can not teach and train you into being a true capable and invisible Soldier as the real soldiers of the world actually are?

This is by no means saying that it is wrong to be where you're at and to be a member of that which you are in that is called a gang what is being specifically expressed is that there is something wrong with the reasoning behind why and how you do what you do.

How so? Because the real killers of the world all have political and social perceptions and concepts that define the reason behind their killings.